THE
BITCH WALL

The Vietnam Wailing Wall

The Bitch Wall was alive with Vietnam psychedelic war graffiti created by American soldiers. It allowed them to express their fears, joys, and hopes. They painted a plywood wall white in a bunker and before it was dry, they began writing war graffiti with magic markers and paint. What started out as a complete joke became the heart and soul of the unit. The wall reflected their lives.

The unit was assigned to defend other combat units so they could move south to safety before the monsoon season. They accomplished their almost impossible mission, but the monsoons came early, before they could return to their base camp. Now their unit was stuck defenseless in the middle of the jungle with mud above their knees and short on food and clean drinking water.

Without warning, the Air Force began bombing their perimeter nonstop with napalm. With everyone standing in formation, the Big Brass arrived and gave a state-side spit-and-polish inspection in the middle of the battlefield. The unit was demoralized. As soon as the Brass left, the protective bombing stopped, and the unit received a message from headquarters alerting them that they were completely surrounded by the Vietcong. Everyone knew that some of them would die that evening. Alone in the jungle, with no place to turn, each man must face his own mortality.

THE BITCH WALL TELLS IT ALL

THE
BITCH-WALL

The Vietnam Wailing Wall

DENNIS LANE

RAMBLE HOUSE

2014

I would like to give special thanks to Francis M. Nevins, Tom Nagel, Paul Moussine and Chelsea Myers for their assistance in editing, creating *The Vietnam Wailing Wall* website and setting up the social media to assist in promoting the book. This had to be established prior to the publication to respond appropriately to the demands of today's complicated self-marketing. Without their assistance, this project would not have been completed. Finally, I also want to thank Fender Tucker and Gavin L. O'Keefe for holding my hand throughout the final preparations of the publication of *The Bitch Wall*.

Dennis Lane

ISBN13: 978-1-60543-803-0

Edited by Dennis Lane and Fender Tucker

Cover Art by Tom Nagel
Cover Design by Gavin L. O'Keefe

Chapter I: DESTINATION VIETNAM

ON THE FLIGHT TO VIETNAM, Bill Freeze was going over in his mind the last few days at home. Even more than the farewell at the airport he remembered his last night out with his closest friends from high school a few days ago.

Three boys and two girls were jammed into a yellow VW Bug. Everyone except Bill was dressed in hippie garb: tie-dyed t-shirts, bell-bottomed jeans, long hair, beards, beads and barefoot. He looked out of place with his friends with his close-cropped hair and clean-shaven appearance, but that night he avoided thinking about leaving for Vietnam in two days. It was great being with his closest friends.

Around midnight, after a movie and pizza, they were taking Bill home first. They wanted to say goodbye to him together. Everyone was having a great time. As they were turning a corner in the Bug, out of nowhere a lighted wooden construction fence jumped out in front of them.

On the fence was written…

Old soldiers never die— young ones do.

Bill's friends continued on, not knowing what to say. *Sergeant Pepper's Lonely Hearts Club Band* blared from the 8-track stereo.

Then the irony of it hit Bill all at once and he laughed loudly. It was now impossible for them to escape from what his departure meant to them.

"I can't even allow myself to think that you might not return like Chris McLaughlin. I honestly couldn't handle you not coming back too!" one of the girls blurted. She hugged Bill and began to cry convulsively.

Nothing else was said until they dropped Bill off. Everyone jumped out of the Bug to say goodbye. No one wanted to leave so they moved spontaneously to the front porch and talked nonstop until sunrise. They knew it was time to leave when they heard Bill's parents stirring in the kitchen around 7:00 A.M.

That final night with his childhood friends would always haunt him.

The roar of jet engines brought Bill back to the plane, and he suddenly found himself on the flight to Vietnam. Though Bill was smiling the entire time, tears were quietly streaming down his face. Several hours passed. He looked at his watch and realized that in only two hours they would be landing in Vietnam. A stewardess inconspicuously placed some Kleenex in his hand.

"Thank you," Bill said as she walked away.

A seasoned soldier was sitting next to Bill. He was returning for his second tour of duty. The soldier told him that everything would be okay but he did not look to be much older than Bill.

Bill asked, "Were you scared the first time going over?"

"I can't even tell you how frightened I was the first time. I'm with the Special Forces." He paused and looked away. "If I knew what I know now I think I would have escaped to Canada."

He caught himself looking Bill straight in the eyes and said, "It's not so bad; you'll be just fine." Then he turned away and didn't say another word.

~ ~ ~ ~ ~

It was a rainy day at the Knoxville airport. Tim Edmonds was a twenty-two year old black man and a 6' 3" physical specimen with a well-muscled body from years of hard manual labor. At sixteen he had dropped out of high school to support Annie when she became pregnant.

Tim had been an athlete in high school. He had planned on living the American dream by earning an athletic scholarship to college and playing professional basketball for the Boston Celtics. Then he accepted the responsibility of a family. Throughout their six years of marriage he deeply regretted that he'd never been able to offer his family the stable living they deserved. He could only offer a day laborer's meager income.

In some ways Annie was relieved that he was leaving for Vietnam. Tim had been involved in repeated fights with his friends at a local bar. Every one of his friends had been in trouble with the law numerous times. One night he had gotten drunk and single-handedly destroyed the place. The judge had offered Tim the option of entering the service or time in jail. After only five months in the Army, Annie had to admit that it already had made a difference.

While he was home on leave before his departure for Vietnam, she noticed that Tim carefully avoided friends. But she had no illusions about him remaining faithful while he was gone. She was more concerned that he did not become a drug addict, an alcoholic or both.

"I will not allow myself to think about Tim not returning. The children adore him—especially our son. I will do my best to take care of them while he is gone," she thought as they walked through the airport on the day of his departure. Their two children ran and played beside them.

She said to Tim, smiling, "You'd think the children were going to Disneyland, the way they're enjoying themselves. I'm glad we came as a family and got to visit an airport."

"Annie, keep care of those two. I'm sorry I won't be here to help you with raising the children during the next year," Tim said tenderly.

"How can you worry about such a thing at a time like this? You know I'm heartsick with worry for you." Annie pulled away from him, grabbed a Kleenex out of her purse and wiped her eyes.

"I'm sorry if I upset you, honey. Annie, you'll never be out of my thoughts."

She looked at him and smiled. "Do you think for one minute that I doubted that?"

The loudspeaker announced the first call for his flight.

Tim kneeled down to speak lovingly to his children. "Georgia, be a good girl for your mother. You hear?" She shook her head yes and kissed her father's cheek.

"Johnnie," he said to his six year old son, "now you are going have to help your mother with me gone. You watch out for both of them. Okay?"

Johnnie smiled. Tim playfully punched his arm, shook his hand, pulled him close, smiled and gave him a kiss on his forehead. Then he turned to Annie. "Lord, I love you. I'm sorry for all my nonsense but I really do love you." She broke down crying. He embraced her and held her and added, "With all the love in my soul."

The startled children ran to them, crying and trying to reach their arms desperately around their father's legs. Tim thought, "I may never see my family again."

The loudspeaker boomed again. "Last call for the flight to Seattle."

Tim began pulling himself away from his family but they clung tighter to him and would not let go. With all his strength he smiled and looked into Annie's eyes one last time and said tenderly, "I have to go."

Gently taking his children's arms from his legs, he placed his kids next to their mother.

"Stand together so I can remember you just the way you are right now. I'm proud of all of you. I love you." He smiled through his tears, then turned abruptly and left.

He headed for the plane, not turning around to look. He thought, "I will run back and not have the strength to leave again."

Georgia hysterically called out to him, "Daddy, Daddy, Daddy!"

Rushing to the plane, Tim heard them calling. Finding a seat, he put his hands over his face. A stewardess delivered a Budweiser and said, "Here, soldier, it's on us. If you want anything else, please just ask."

Unable to speak, Tim nodded as she walked away quickly down the narrow aisle of the packed commercial flight of people in business suits and families going on vacations. He thought, "It's obvious that I'm the only one going to Vietnam."

The stewardess wouldn't forget seeing him and his family clinging to each other, and she wondered, hardly containing herself, if he would ever see his family again. She thought, "This beautiful young soldier on his journey to a place whose name brings terror to my soul." Like most Americans, she had seen the horrifying images on television.

It was almost impossible for Tim to calm himself down. He could not stop thinking about his family and how much he loved them. But an hour after takeoff, Tim eventually gained some control. Cracking open the can of beer, he threw his head back. "Fuck it. Next stop Fort Lewis . . . then Vietnam."

~ ~ ~ ~ ~

While driving to the San Francisco airport, Dan Semple's father thought, "I anticipated my only child would eventually accept the position as heir to our family company, instead of running off to this so-called police action. It does not even qualify as a legitimate war. I know I have been an absentee father. However, he has never appreciated my passion for business. This is the legacy that I am leaving him."

However, in many ways Dan was exactly like his father, and neither one knew how to make amends after years without communication. Mr. Semple depended on his wife to resolve the tension somehow. But neither Dan nor his girlfriend Cathy responded to her awkward attempts at discussion on the trip in their Mercedes to the airport. Mrs. Semple thought that if Cathy wasn't there, perhaps she could have communicated.

It was the first time Dan's parents had met Cathy. Dan had met her in undergraduate school at Stanford University. The irony was that Cathy also desperately wanted to communicate with Dan but felt completely shut out of his insular world.

Dan was a slightly built 22-year old with blonde hair and blue eyes. He looked a bit like a mouse. He had learned early in life that he could excel intellectually but never compete athletically. If asked, his classmates would say they remembered Dan for always carrying a pile of books. Although Dan had never verbalized it to anyone, he wanted to go to Vietnam to overcome his lack of confidence. His classmates would have thought that he was the least likely to go to war and serve in a combat unit.

There was no turning back now. He wondered if he had made the right decision, but he would not allow himself to think about that right now. All he knew was the crisis in which he'd put himself.

When they arrived at the airport, Dan and Cathy walked ahead of his parents, just out of hearing range.

"Why did they have to come, Dan?" Cathy said with contempt.

"I tried to tell them but I was afraid of hurting them. At least I got the rest of my grandparents, aunts, uncles, and cousins to stay at home. For some reason everyone wanted to come."

"Yeah, I suppose you're right, Dan. I never said this before, but I love you and will miss you while you are gone. I'm embarrassed." After a pause, "At least I have my graduate assistantship at Stanford to occupy me while you're gone."

"I want to thank you for these past six months. I think the year will go quickly. Maybe we should talk to my parents now."

He turned to them. "Mom and Dad, you know that according to Army regulations if I return home from Vietnam with three months or less of active duty, I can get an automatic early out. If my unit is in a safe position, I will extend my tour of duty in Vietnam so I can get the early-out. I'd rather be there than finishing my obligation bored on a base stateside doing nothing. I want to be clear. I'll try to get out of the Army as soon as possible, even if that means more time in Vietnam."

Then Dan blurted out unexpectedly, "Also, I know I graduated with honors to succeed in business. But I guess I never believed that I could measure up to your expectations. That's why I'm going."

"I don't know why you're doing this!" his father replied with shock and anger. "Even now I can do something to help you get out of the service. You don't have to do this! Danny, why haven't you thought about Canada like other young men? At least you'd be safe!"

Dan turned to Cathy and they exchanged pained looks.

"This is my life. I have to do what I think is best. When will you understand that? It's simple enough, isn't it?"

"You have every right to decide what you want to do with your life. But Vietnam? Dan, wars don't make any sense. This one makes less sense! We just want what is best for you. Over there..." She sobbed. "You've got nothing to prove by going over there."

"All my life you've interfered. I'm boarding the plane early. You can stay here. Good-bye!" Dan yelled back.

He turned to Cathy. "I'll write you. Take care of yourself." He hugged her and gave her a quick kiss on the cheek. Then abruptly, without saying good-bye to his parents, he left.

Cathy was distressed with Dan's abrupt departure. She turned to Dan's parents. "I need to be alone."

She walked to a window past the rows of empty seats and stared out at the large commercial airliner until the plane backed out and taxied down the tarmac.

Mr. Semple turned to his wife and whispered with his lips close to her cheek, "Martha, I don't believe he really knows what he's getting himself into. He'll be completely out of his element over there. All that math and philosophy he learned in college isn't going to do him any good in combat." He looked into her eyes and put his arms around her and said, "We'd better go home."

But they had to wait another half hour for Cathy. They watched her staring out the window. Then they rode back to their home on Nob Hill in almost unbearable silence. Everyone refused to initiate a conversation.

~ ~ ~ ~ ~

Nineteen-year-old Bill Freeze was waiting silently at LaGuardia airport with his parents, grandmother, two sisters, little brother, and Amanda and George McLaughlin.

Bill was an extraordinarily handsome young man, six feet, dark brown curly hair, blue eyes, and a flawless complexion. At nineteen, his face lacked any traces of hair. In spite of his physical presence he was completely unaware of how he affected others.

He had always excelled academically throughout school and earned a full scholarship to Yale, but during the second semester of his freshman year his best friend Chris McLaughlin had died in Vietnam. On hearing this news he had dropped out and volunteered for the draft.

Chris was gregarious and everyone had loved him. Unlike Bill, he hated school, and signed up for the draft. He had entered the U.S. Army two weeks after high school graduation but had served with the infantry for only six months when he stepped on a land mine.

Chris had returned home in a closed coffin, and both families had lost a son when he died. He had seemed invincible. It had been less than a year since his death.

Chris's mom had said to Bill's mother, "Elaine, I wish he didn't feel he had to go to Vietnam because of what happened to Chris. It's been so difficult for everyone. I just wish we could have had more children. I'm sure that would have made it easier."

"I know we loved Chris as if he were our own son," Mrs. Freeze responded. "I know Bill will never get over it. I just wish he'd waited a little longer before signing up. Nothing would stop him, Joan. They were inseparable growing up. I'm so glad you've been our neighbor for all these years."

"We'll always be grateful how wonderful the members of your congregation were. The support from your church was wonderful for our family," said Mrs. Freeze. "Because we're immigrants and don't have any family in this country, we would have been alone without your family's wonderful support. I'll never be able to thank you enough."

"I know you would have done the same thing for us. Don't worry about it. It's been almost impossible for us to talk about Chris. I can hardly think about it without crying. We love your family so much," said Mrs. McLaughlin. "It was because of their friendship that our families have grown so close through the years. I can't express to you how much your friendship means to us."

They walked out of range because they didn't want the others to see that they were both crying.

Although there was no exchange between the fathers, both of them felt deeply indebted to America as immigrants. Chris' family were Irish Catholic and Bill's were Eastern European Jews. They believed that it was their sons' moral responsibility to defend their country.

As the time got closer for Bill to leave, everyone was waiting in complete silence.

Finally Bill's mother spoke. "Son, the family will be praying for you constantly while you're gone. Everyone at our temple knows you're going to Vietnam and will be praying for you too." As she looked over to Chris' mother fondly, "A candle will always be burning in your honor at the McLaughlins' church until you return home safely."

Bill looked at his mother. She started crying when he looked her in the eyes. "Mom, I love you. I hope you understand that this is something I have to do. I'd never forgive myself if I didn't have the courage to do this. I know Chris would have done the same thing."

"We understand. I hope you realize how much everyone loves you." They clutched each other.

Finally Bill's youngest brother, seven-year-old Adam, ran over to him crying. "Oh, Bill, come back to me, please. I'll miss you. I'm afraid you won't come back like Chris." Everyone took a deep breath at his honesty.

Bill picked up Adam and held him close, trying to calm him down. The rest of the family watched helplessly. Then he gently placed his inconsolable little brother into his grandmother's arms and kissed her on the cheek.

Finally he looked at his best friend's parents, smiled, and walked over to them. The McLaughlins embraced Bill and began sobbing. He gave them both a kiss and thanked them for coming.

The loudspeaker boomed. "Last call for Flight 711 to Seattle."

Bill rushed to his plane. He turned one last time, took a lingering look at those he loved, smiled, and held up the peace sign before entering the plane.

~ ~ ~ ~ ~

Eighteen-year-old Bobby Swenson, his parents, and some of his high school football buddies were sauntering through the El Paso airport. No one seemed concerned about his final destination. Bobby had grown up an army brat and lived throughout the world on military bases until his parents retired to a small ranch in west Texas near El Paso.

He was captain of the football team, a notoriously heavy drinker who screwed any girl who succumbed to his rugged good looks and macho charms. West Texas, he thought, was the land of the stompers. They were always ready to stomp anyone's ass who was not white, Protestant and dared to get in their way.

"I want you to go over there and kill every gook you see, just like I killed every fucking Jap, kraut or dago I could in World War II and the Korean War. I am proud of you, son, carrying on our military tradition," Mr. Swenson said to Bobby at the terminal.

"You know I'll make you proud, Dad. I'll kill every Vietcong that gets in my way. It's my goal to match your two Purple Hearts and Bronze Stars. I'll hang 'em in our living room," Bobby responded excitedly.

"Oh Bobby, I just want you to come home safe," Mrs. Swenson interjected into their conversation. "I don't care if you've earned any combat medals. Just come back. The members of our church will be praying for you every day."

Mr. Swenson was furious. "What the hell are you doing pushing that Christian fundamentalist bullshit at a time like this? He doesn't need to hear that now. We need to let him know that we believe in him, that he's going to make us proud."

While listening to another of her husband's tirades, she had decided to leave him if anything happened to her youngest child. Once ten years ago she had separated from him for physical abuse. If there were a second time she would not return now that the children were grown. For years her daughters had been begging her to leave him.

For Bobby's sake she contained her emotions at the airport, but his friends completely ignored her. They were even more excited about Bobby's departure because of Mr. Swenson's legacy.

"Well, Momma, I'll be gone just twelve months. I'll be back before you know it," Bobby said light-heartedly.

She was almost speechless. "Oh, Bobby, you'll never be out of my thoughts and prayers while you're gone."

"Come back and make me proud, son. Kill all the slant-eyed bastards you can for me." He slapped Bobby proudly on the back.

"You know I won't let you down, Dad."

"I know you won't, son." He was smiling proudly at Bobby.

"My brother was over there and he said it ain't bad at all! No way!" bragged one of his high school buddies.

"Yeah, you'll get lots of free beer. And you'll get to screw all the slant-eyed bitches you want. Wow, I kind of envy you!" jumped in another. His friends laughed.

"Yeah, show 'em what a good ole boy is made of. None of them can fight like us."

"I showed 'em in two wars, son. Now it's your turn to show 'em in Vietnam. There's nobody as tough as the men from west Texas," his father said.

The loudspeaker announced the last call for his plane.

"Well, I better go." He saluted his father and his friends. The boys returned his salute. Then he looked at his mother.

Mrs. Swenson was grief stricken. "Bobby, just come home." She reached out to kiss him. He gave her a quick kiss and abruptly boarded the plane.

~ ~ ~ ~ ~

In April the sky is almost always dark and overcast, and a constant mist makes Fort Lewis, Washington damp and unbearable. It was the primary base to ship men to Vietnam, and for the lucky ones, it returned them home again. The atmosphere was heavy with people coming and going.

On arrival Bobby, Tim, Bill and Dan, along with other soldiers, were checked in, processed through, and transported to Vietnam on a classy commercial airliner.

World Airlines was a harsh contrast to the dingy military base they had just left and an even sharper contrast to their final destination. It was like a cruel joke to be flown over in such luxury. It didn't make any sense to anyone, but they enjoyed the free beer.

The stewardesses were well aware of the absurdity of the situation. They were beautiful young women from different countries with varied accents. The passengers desired them. But the women had seen many soldiers on their flight over to

Vietnam. Some even recognized the same faces on their flight back. When they observed a soldier on the way home, he had lost something. The women could not begin to comprehend what the young men had lost or why. Was it their boyhood naiveté? Or was it that they had watched their friends die and lost the ability to connect emotionally with anyone again? It was frightening. These women could not reconcile how Vietnam destroyed youthful vitality and filled their passengers with despair. They taught themselves not to question and only to serve with efficiency.

About halfway through the flight, Bobby Swenson put on the call light for a stewardess. She came immediately.

"I'd like to order an ice cold Budweiser. I'm not sure how long it will be before I can get a cold one again," he said with the smile he used to charm all the women.

"I have to ask for your military ID to make sure that you are twenty-one years old," she said.

"What the hell are you talking about? If I'm old enough to go off to fight in a war for my country, I'm sure in hell gonna drink a beer. This doesn't make any fucking sense."

"Sir, I don't make the rules but I have to follow them. I sorry and I agree with you that I should be able to serve you a beer. Unfortunately, I can't or I'd lose my job," the stewardess said helplessly.

A young sergeant sitting next to Bobby ordered two beers. He winked at Bobby and whispered, "Don't worry, you'll get whatever you want. Just learn how to play the game. Remember, the key is never to get caught."

Bobby smiled back. "Thanks."

The stewardess knew this trick and was relieved that someone had come to Bobby's rescue. She brought the sergeant two beers. As soon as she walked away, he handed one to Bobby. They toasted to who would kill the most fucking slant-eyed gooks in the next twelve months. And they promised to stay in contact so they could keep score.

After a few more beers a stewardess announced over the speaker, "Please fasten your belts and place your seats in an upright position. We will be landing shortly in Cam Ranh Bay, Vietnam. We are very proud to have served you." She paused before saying, "We look forward to serving you again in the future."

Chapter 2: THE BLUR OF DAY ONE

THE U.S. ARMY was the ultimate equalizer, choosing men indiscriminately from all walks of life and throwing them together. It obliged them to work and live as a unit, army indoctrinating with green uniforms, tropical combat boots, ill-prepared chow, filthy shower stalls, fornication in whorehouses, defecation in cropped-off drums filled with diesel fuel. Each soldier's unique heritage and traditions were put aside to survive in military conformity. Combat troops in Vietnam referred to everything else as "the world".

The men were checked in, processed and made ready to be delivered to A Battery base camp only 48 hours after leaving their homes. They found themselves waiting in another airport and caught up in the treadmill of Vietnam.

Phu Cat Air Force Base was located in south central Vietnam 20 miles from the South China Sea. The men were segregated at base camp and groups randomly selected to serve in the same unit. When they arrived, they were escorted to the tent where they would be spending their first night together.

No one had spoken, and as they examined their new surroundings silently on their cots, the supply sergeant burst into the tent.

Terrified, they jumped to attention. He smiled and said, "At ease, men. This is Vietnam. Relax and sit down. Someone from your unit will be coming to pick you up at 1000 hours tomorrow. I'd advise you to hit the nightclub on the base tonight. Raise some hell. It'll be awhile before you are back in civilization again. You'll need to report to me no later than 0900 hours tomorrow. If you need me, I'll be in the tent where you checked in when you first arrived. Try not to let this place get to you. Good luck."

He smiled and left.

"I don't know about you guys, but I'm fucking hungry," Bobby said. "Let's go get some chow."

Dan agreed.

As they were leaving the tent Tim spoke. "Aren't you guys forgetting something? We have to bring our gear with us wherever we go now." They grabbed their helmets and M-16 rifles.

"This is going to take some getting used to, carrying this war paraphernalia with us wherever we go," Bill joked.

"I like it. I feel like John Wayne," Bobby said. They laughed and headed to the mess tent.

After dinner they hunted for the enlisted men's nightclub. It was easy to identify them as green troops since they casually asked anyone who passed by for directions. Seasoned troops stared as they sauntered by in relaxed formation.

When they found the nightclub, they heard an Asian band playing Beatles music. The combination created a surreal concoction but no one cared. They were following the supply sergeant's instructions and going to raise some hell.

Bobby was elated. "Let me buy the first round. You know, I never figured there'd be anything like this in Vietnam. Hey, waitress."

A pretty young Vietnamese girl came over to their table.

"Four Budweisers!" he barked.

A few hours earlier they had had heavy hearts, but a frivolous atmosphere permeated the nightclub. They talked for hours, drinking non-stop.

The conversation was mostly about home. They found out that they had all trained for the artillery at Fort Sill, Oklahoma. In fact they had been there at the same time but their paths had never crossed.

They wondered why. But it made no difference. They were having a great time getting incoherent.

"This compensates for whatever will be ahead. Tonight is the last night we'll be able to celebrate as if we don't have a care in the world," Dan said, trying to analyze the atmosphere.

After the bar closed they walked back to their tent. The tents they passed glowed red. They stopped and listened to the music blaring from each section's living quarters: Acid Rock, Country Western, Folk, Classical, and Soul. Through the translucent canvas walls of the tents they saw the silhouettes of men laughing and talking.

When they heard Aretha Franklin singing "Respect", they stopped and sang with Lady Soul. They danced wildly.

> *R-E-S-P-E-C-T find out what that means to me,*
> *R-E-S-P-E-C-T take out the TCP (Sock it to me, Sock it to me . . .,*
> *A little respect oh yeah, (Just a little bit...)*
> *A little respect oh yeah. (Just a little bit...)*

Suddenly the music stopped and there was total silence. Coming to their senses, Bill, Dan, Tim and Bobby were alone. In the quiet of the night they looked up at the tropical sky above Phu Cat.

"I've never seen so many stars in the sky in my life. In Manhattan, most nights you can't even see the stars," Bill said. He was in awe.

They examined the lights in amazement for another half hour. Then they walked back to their tent in silence. They had to prepare for tomorrow's 30 mile journey to A Battery. That night they couldn't believe that they would be living in a combat zone for the next 12 months. If they did believe it, everyone would bolt.

~ ~ ~ ~ ~

The next morning all four were hung over. They waited for the truck from A Battery to pick them up early in the morning.

"Well, fuck, men, we're finally heading to our unit, and I am excited. I heard that it's the best unit in 1st Field Forces. That means they must think that we're among the top killers here," Bobby said proudly, still buzzed.

"I'm not sure that any of us measure up really. It may just be the luck of the draw. I think it also means that we'll be called to go on special missions, and that shit scares the hell out of me," Dan added.

"I say to the four of you, I think we'll be fine. At this point I don't think we should worry about a fucking thing." Bobby patted Dan on the back and smiled at him.

The truck from A Battery was running late. They had to wait another hour until 1100. They grew silent. It was an intolerably hot and humid day. Tim offered everyone a cigarette. Bobby took one. Then the two of them began discussing how they would hook up with some of those beautiful slant-eyed women they had heard so much about. They made gestures. Dan and Bill just sat in the dirt drinking from their canteens.

"For the first time I can totally relate to President Eisenhower's farewell speech. I feel like I'm caught up in the military industrial complex and there's nothing I can do about it," Bill said. He was fatigued.

Dan nodded in agreement.

Finally in the distance a two ton truck gunned toward them. Dust streamed behind it in a long bilious cloud. The truck drew closer. Two men in the cab pulled it in directly in front of them. One jumped out.

"So these are our new recruits?" He eyed them over. "It's damn good to see you men in our midst. You are now part of the illustrious A Battery. Be prepared for the worst. In the past two weeks alone we've had four dead and nine wounded, with various degrees of seriousness." He said this in a thick New York accent.

The other man was angry. "Caldwell, shut the fuck up." He looked at the four new recruits. "It's just not as bad as he'd like you to think." He put out his hand and said warmly, "Hello, I'm Specialist 4 George Morrison, but everyone calls me Flower Power. I'm the unit's token flower child from sunny Southern California." He pointed to Caldwell. "My obnoxious friend Phil Caldwell is obviously from the Bronx."

Caldwell was unruffled. "You men are lucky because today we're going on one of our infamous ammo runs."

"Everyone throw your gear in the back of the truck and pile in," Flower Power said. "I'll ride with the new recruits. Anyone want to ride shotgun with Caldwell?"

"Hell, yes!" Bobby volunteered. He jumped into the cab of the truck.

"I'm going to check in with the supply sergeant to see if there's anything to take back to the unit," Caldwell said. He ran into the supply tent, came back with their orders, jumped into the cab, and they took off flying down the road for the ammo dump.

They were officially off U.S. territory for the first time. None of them had seen anything like it before. They passed a little village outside the gates of the base. Some of the Vietnamese on the road cursed them and gave them the finger. Bobby observed that Caldwell seemed to be aiming right for them. They scurried out of the way.

"These are the people we were sent to defend?" Tim said to the others in the truck bed. He had learned at the bar last night that any typical border village offered every sensual delight a soldier could desire. On the road below the truck, the vendors were selling jewelry, clothing, and American cigarettes.

People crowded the streets. They walked alongside the truck. Bobby, riding shotgun, watched the women with children walking in the middle of the street, slowing down the traffic so the mama-sans could bring hundreds of items to the truck to sell.

Phil Caldwell explained to Bobby. "It's nearing the end of the month, another week before payday. So everything is cheap. They sell with more and more intensity the closer it comes to the end of the month. But once payday comes, man, prices shoot up! This is the free market system at work. Even with all this enticement, I don't buy nothing from these fucking foreign vendors."

Bobby tried to identify with Caldwell. "Yeah, at the night club on base they gooked up the rock-and-roll too."

Once out of the tiny village, the men in back watched the passing rice paddies that extended for miles and the lush green mountains in the distance.

"They look like an Asian watercolor artist painted them," Flower Power said to Dan as they stared from the back of the truck.

It was a short trip to Qui Nohn to pick up the ammo. The truck was signed out until 1600 hours. But the new recruits didn't understand why the trip would take so long since it was only 1100 hours. They had been told that it would take only an hour and a half to drive back to their new unit.

The ammo for the eight-inch cannons was picked up in less than an hour. Leaving the ammo dump, Caldwell didn't seem to head towards the unit but to the center of Qui Nohn, located on the South China Sea.

Flower Power explained to Dan. "Before the American occupation, this served as a resort for the colonial settlers, and the beaches are as beautiful as those on the French Riviera. Qui Nohn City still retains a French Provincial flavor."

Caldwell drove through the crowded streets with amazing dexterity. He said to Bobby, "I have memorized this destination."

He pulled into a secure parking lot in town that was guarded by the military police. Caldwell put the truck in park and ran to the back. "Now we're going to separate the men from the boys," he announced.

"What is he talking about?" said Tim to Dan.

Flower Power shook his head. "He means who wants to have their first experience with the slant-eyed women? Caldwell, why don't you fuck off? They don't even understand what this hellhole is all about yet."

"If you want to come with me, let's go!" Caldwell barked wildly.

Bobby and Tim jumped out of the truck and followed Caldwell, who was playing tour guide. Dan and Bill hung back with Flower Power.

"I figured that you two were my kind of guys. I'm going to show you one of the best whorehouses in Qui Nohn City. It's 'The French Riviera Beauties, Inc.' But let me give you a piece of advice. Choose one of the uglier girls, because no one else wants to fuck them. They're cleaner. Get me? If you get one of the better looking whores, the odds are pretty high that she's got the clap or something."

"Or the Black Syph?" Bobby Swenson asked.

"So you've heard of our infamous Black Syph?" Caldwell laughed.

"What the hell is the Black Syph?" Tim Edmonds asked.

"It's a strain of VD that's so tough, so mean, that not even penicillin or all the antibiotics in the world can cure it," Caldwell said with delight and a cringe.

Tim was taken aback. "What happens to you if you get it?"

"The story goes that they send you off to an island in the South Pacific somewhere and you're never heard from again." Caldwell added with a serious note: "Oh, and your parents get a letter from the Army stating that their son died while in the service of his country."

Tim and Bobby had worried faces.

"Oh, don't be concerned about it. I've never met anyone who caught it yet."

Caldwell paused, enjoying his own humor.

"But, man, this soldier ain't gonna wear any boot when I'm screwing one of these hot whorehouse girls. Oh, by the way, boot is slang for a rubber here," Caldwell said. "Don't worry about it."

They found themselves in front of "The French Riviera Beauties, Inc." The large dilapidated old building looked as if it might have been a small department store during the French occupation.

Inside Tim, Bobby and Phil found a cramped lobby with an older Vietnamese woman waiting behind the counter. It was furnished with cheap, bright blue and orange plastic furniture. The air was clogged with the smell of cheap perfume and stale cum. Incense was burning to cover both odors.

"It only serves to make the combination of the different odors more intolerable. It smells sweet but not clean," Caldwell explained in a reassuring voice.

"Hello, GIs, can I help you, please?" the old woman with the sun-dried skin at the counter said with a knowing smile, and young girls poured into the cramped lobby from every direction and doorway. Tim and Bobby stood there anxiously anticipating their first Vietnam lay as they drew close. The girls rubbed them and crowded around them. Caldwell stood back watching the newbies' reactions as the girls made their sales pitch.

"Fix me up with my girl, Laura. And take good care of my friends, it's their first time." He left and entered the hallway behind a curtain made from flip-tops and beer cans strung together. "I'll meet you guys back here at 1500 hours," he said before disappearing.

"Fuck Caldwell's advice about choosing an ugly girl," Tim said to Bobby. Tim smiled and nodded.

Lou Ann was a beautiful young woman, a mix of French and Vietnamese. She smiled and rubbed Tim's crotch. He smiled back at her. She extended her delicate hand and led him to a makeshift bedroom and closed the curtain.

That was when Tim thought about Annie and his children. He had left just two days ago.

Lou Ann stopped him, smiled. "You afraid, GI? Maybe you a virgin?"

"Hell no, I am no fucking virgin. I have been with a lot of women. I am known as the best."

"Then maybe you show me. Will I be your first Vietnamese girl? You know I will be the best," she smiled. She rubbed him up again and led him to the bed.

Tim forgot about everything but relieving himself. Lou Ann took off her clothes, lay on her back on the bed and spread her legs. Tim walked to the bed and pulled off his pants. After she lubricated him, she directed him to her open loins. Then he started frantically pounding her.

In the middle of the action Tim had one last brief thought of Annie. "She should have known that I couldn't keep faithful for very long. Fuck it. I'm going to have a good time while I'm here. I can't stay away from pussy my entire time in Vietnam."

~ ~ ~ ~ ~

Meanwhile, Flower Power was giving Bill Freeze and Dan Semple a guided tour of Qui Nohn City.

"I want to show you some of the different market places and the beach. If you have the time, the exotic atmosphere can entrance you. The Qui Nohn City streets are even more crowded than the border town next to the base. People are buying and selling goods everywhere. The war has made some of the Vietnamese very prosperous. But it's a prosperity that isn't welcomed by everyone. This corruption was created by the war."

A boy street vendor ran up to Dan. "American, you want buy watch?"

Dan stopped to look. "Hey, this isn't bad. It's a Seiko. How much?" Dan's father owned an electronics company in San Francisco. He knew all the brands well. This was an area he'd specialized when studying business in undergraduate school. But he had left for Vietnam because he had wanted to prove something.

"Whatever it is, it's too much," Flower Power immediately interrupted, grabbing the watch and inspecting it. "See where it says 17-jewel watch? Well, they take all the jewels out except for those that are needed to keep the watch running until you get back to the unit. With the other jewels they make jewelry." He threw it back to the boy. "Now get out of here!"

The boy ran away but turned around. "You cheap GIs. You all number fucking ten."

Flower Power laughed. "Number ten means we're bad news. Now, if we were okay we'd be number one, if you know what I mean."

Dan and Bill didn't understand.

"For example, Raquel Welch is number one and that means she's great. And Phyllis Diller would be a number ten because she's so fucking ugly. Anyway, we rate everything on a scale from one to ten here. Get used to it now," Flower Power explained.

They browsed the different shops. Dan was distant and quiet. The other two said nothing. Flower Power figured Dan must be having a rough time. Their hangovers were finally wearing off. They came up to an alley and on the wall:

> There are 6 or 7 acceptable ways to win this war 2 or 3 unacceptable ones, and only one way to lose it and we have found it.

"I imagine that was written by someone who knows the whole story here," Bill said.

"Don't let it get you down. You see American graffiti like that, even worse, everywhere you go here. Even the Vietnamese write on the walls. We can't read it, but I bet it's no different than ours except they probably hate most of us," Flower Power explained.

"I suppose you're right. It's just that I can't imagine why we're here defending these people. The domino theory suddenly looks pretty flimsy to me where one country falls to communism and another and another," said Dan.

"Let's go to the beach," Flower Power interjected emphatically. He fetched a taxi, which was a motor scooter with a small compartment attached to the back. It was large enough for only one of them but they piled in.

"Body surfing in the afternoon sun, Bill and Dan, you might even forget what lies ahead in just a few hours. Even you, Dan, seem to be in better shape now," Flower Power said in the cab.

"I had no idea that I'd be swimming the South China Sea my first week in Vietnam," Bill responded.

"Yeah, well, enjoy it while you can," Flower Power said.

"Between last night and today I'm not sure what to think," Dan added.

"It'll become all too clear soon enough," Flower Power said reassuringly.

At the beach Bill and Flower Power ran into the sea and enjoyed the rest of the afternoon playing in the water like two small children who didn't want to leave.

"You guys go ahead. I want to spend the rest of my time reading and relaxing in the sun," Dan said as the two called to him from the surf.

He couldn't concentrate on his reading. He was regretting his farewell to his parents and Cathy.

He thought, "Why did I have to be so callous with my parents? For the first time in years, my father came to my bedroom and attempted to have an actual conversation with me. He was trying to make amends with me before I left for Vietnam. He was almost speechless; his words were barely audible. As much as I wanted to respond, I was incapable because of all the years of lack of communication with him." He was staring out at the other two soldiers splashing like children in the ocean.

"Then there's my mother. She's always been supportive no matter what I was involved in. She let me know how proud she was of me throughout my life. If I'd responded to either one of them, I would have lost all self control. Under no circumstances would this have been acceptable. I got myself in this foolish mess because I had to prove to everyone that I was independent from them. The U.S. Army is the one place I knew that they couldn't interfere." He closed his paperback and stared out at the eastern horizon where San Francisco was thousands of miles away.

"Finally there's Cathy. No woman has ever told me that she loved me before. It was unexpected. I ignored what she said." He whispered this last part.

He took a deep breath, calming himself so that he did not cry, and thought: "If I do see them again, will I have the emotional stability to let them know how much I love them?

I doubt it. I should write a letter. As much as I would like, I can't communicate my feelings through something as distant as a letter. Why isn't it easier to let people know that you love them?"

Flower Power called Dan. "We better get ready to leave so we can make it back to A Battery before nightfall." They fetched another taxi and returned back to the truck by 1500 hours as planned. Bill and Dan were still wet in their fatigues.

At the secure lot they had to wait until 1625 before the other three returned from their excursion. When Phil Caldwell, Tim Edmonds, and Bobby sauntered back to the parking lot wearing big relaxed smiles, they were stumbling drunk.

"Now, man, don't be angry. We can make it back before dark if we hurry," Caldwell said. His words were slurred and almost incomprehensible with his accent. Flower Power was used to it.

"Hell, yes, you fucking idiot, we'll get back, but we'll have to fucking bust ass to do it. We're already late!" Flower Power barked. "If we're not back in before dark, I'm not taking this rap for you, Caldwell, you dumb mother fucker!"

"Okay, okay, you win," Caldwell said, totally unaffected. Then he laughed. "Here're the keys. You'd better drive!"

"Tell Bill to grab his rifle and come up front to ride shotgun for me," Flower Power responded. They hopped into the front cab and Flower Power gunned it to the unit. Tim, Bobby and Caldwell stretched out in the truck and shut their eyes. Dan watched the dust kick up as the truck rolled out of the city and they hauled ass on the winding dirt roads.

Bill observed the beauty of the countryside. It was more picturesque in the setting of the sun. He watched the Vietnamese working in the rice paddies.

"These people are poor!" Bill shouted over the engine to Flower Power.

"The poverty exists," Flower Power yelled adamantly, "because the countryside has suffered from the ravages of war under the French and Americans. They've been fucked by both occupying nations! That is why I'm going to be a full-time anti-war protester if I ever make it back home again."

It was dusk. Even with the headlights on it was hard to see what was ahead on the road. They sped recklessly through the crowded villages.

Then they heard a loud thud.

Flower Power jumped out and ran to the front to see what he had hit.

"A fucking gook!" he yelled.

He radioed from the truck cab for a helicopter to pick up the old Vietnamese woman lying in the road. "She was carrying food across the road to her family," he said to himself.

Now she was screaming in Vietnamese, crumpled and bleeding, blood pouring from her mouth, eyes, ears and nose.

Bill jumped out of the truck cab to see what was going on. "Is she okay, Flower Power?"

Flower Power was unconcerned. Vietnamese gathered around the truck by the old woman. They were hysterical, traumatized by her twisted bleeding body. She was convulsing. In the chaos of the situation, the Vietnamese hardly even noticed Bill standing there.

Bill was watching Flower Power silently. Flower Power was pissed. He stood with his arms crossed a few feet away from the woman. He wasn't disturbed by the victim or the commotion of the villagers gathered around here.

"The only thing that matters is that this shit will make us even later," Flower Power said calmly.

A helicopter arrived and landed in an open field nearby. Two medics slid the old woman on a stretcher and carried her away. The crowd followed close behind, wailing. Then one of the medics gave a thumbs-up to the pilot of the Medevac Huey and it lifted off the ground over the heads of the wailing villagers.

Bill continued to watch in disbelief. Things were going too fast for him. He was buzzing and overloaded, and it was impossible for him to figure it all out. "Six days ago I was home with my family, he thought, staring at where the helicopter had just vanished over some palm trees."

Bill looked up. Dan was staring at him.

"I have the feeling that this is just the beginning," Dan said cynically.

"Get in the truck, we have to get the fuck out of here," Flower Power yelled. Bill and Dan jumped into the truck bed. Flower Power handed the keys to Caldwell, who had been taking a nap in the truck bed until the crash woke him up.

They bolted down the road. Flower Power sat in the truck bed and pulled out a joint and lit it. "You want some?"

Bill shook his head and they drove on. Flower Power puffed the joint, bouncing up and down in the truck bed as night fell.

When they rolled into A Battery, there was no one in the orderly room. Flower Power rushed to find the company clerk to find out what bunkers they had been assigned. After they were separated and directed to their new living quarters, they were free their first night as a token gesture to the new recruits. Nobody wanted newbies to pull guard duty, protecting them as they slept, or to be assigned to a section on their first night. Tonight they were too tired, and everyone had to worry about tomorrow and the day after.

After days of travel, A Battery was to be their home for twelve months. They found their makeshift living quarters and, exhausted, slept the first night.

Chapter 3: BIRTH OF THE BITCH WALL

THE UNIT, which fired projectiles from cannons 8 inches in diameter, was situated on a hill near Landing Zone Lady. The four artillery pieces in the unit were mobilized on tracks similar to tanks. These were the most accurate artillery weapons, and the men who worked on them were proud.

A Battery had the best reputation of any artillery unit in the 7th Battalion. In fact, it was always selected for review before the generals and colonels when an outstanding example of a firing battery was required. From experience, the combat units in the field learned to depend on this firing machine to get the fucking job done when they wanted their asses to be protected.

The firing battery was laid out as follows:

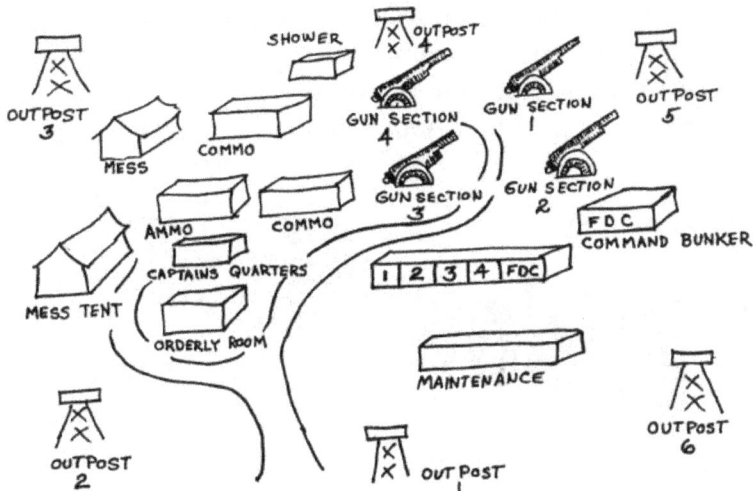

Tim was assigned to the communications section (Commo). Even though he was trained as a cannoneer, he was sent to Commo because it was short-handed. The Army distributed incoming personnel to wherever a warm body was needed. During combat conditions it made no difference in what Military Occupational Specialty (MOS) a soldier had been trained. But Tim was happy. This section was comprised primarily of men who were black or Hispanic.

Commo avoided most of the spit-and-polish which the blacks called honky bo-jive that the other sections had to maintain. But the deliberate segregation of the races into specific sections produced a volatile underlying tension in the unit. Soon enough everyone became numbed to the situation. It had to be ignored if they wanted to survive. Besides, only a fucking idiot would challenge this artificially created status quo.

The Commo section's primary function was to assure that there was telephone communication among the other sections in the unit and to guarantee that there was radio communication with soldiers in the field, especially Headquarters, Battalion and First Field Forces.

Each gun section was responsible for maintaining, aiming, and firing the eight-inch cannons. Bobby, assigned to the 1st Gun Section, was in his glory where he was assigned. In Army tradition, the men in each section christened their gun by selecting a name and painting it on the end of the barrel. The name embodied the mission of each section. The mission of each man in 1st Gun Section was to be a

Widow Maker

This gun section had earned the reputation as the best because it was the fastest and most accurate when expediting a firing operation. It was important to the other troops when the artillery was their only means of support.

Sergeant Chen was the section chief. He was a Chinese American from Chicago whose Asian background aided in leading his multi-racial team of blacks, whites, Hispanics and Asians. But Bobby was not prepared to be treated as an equal with "niggers, wetbacks and slant-eyes."

At the same time, Dan was selected immediately to serve with the fire directional center because of his math background. The section received and deciphered communications for the firing missions from Battalion, Headquarters, forward observers, and other units or platoons. It was imperative for the firing missions that the coordinates be precise. Accurate firing power was needed to defend the other American combat units in the bush by firing lethal hits on the enemy.

The men in this section considered themselves the brains of the outfit. Their intellectual elitism was divisive. The other sections considered these men wimps because they never had to contend with the weather or pull guard duty, and they were usually sheltered from enemy gunfire inside the fire directional bunker. Dan found his element here.

Bill was assigned to the same section. He had been trained to work on the big guns as a cannoneer, but because the fire directional center was short of trained personnel, he was assigned there. He learned quickly and became proficient in the use of the radio and the mathematics for firing the big guns during combat missions. But unlike the others, Bill was unsure if he had been assigned to the right section. He wanted to serve directly in combat like his friend Chris. Bill was spared serving on the line of fire because of his intellectual ability, and he could not completely reconcile himself to his assignment. Still, he was determined to make the best of his placement.

~ ~ ~ ~ ~

Bill, Tim, Bobby, and Dan reported to the orderly room to officially check in and meet the commanding officer, Captain Biddle, and the Chief Non-Commissioned Officer, First Sergeant Long. It was a formality which could have been handled entirely by the company clerk.

"Why is this necessary? It's 0730 in the fucking morning. The first sergeant is still sleeping and Captain Biddle is nowhere," Bobby complained when they showed up at the tent.

"I guess the Army still plays Hurry Up and Wait even in combat," said Dan.

The first sergeant had been up all night drinking with some of his lifer buddies. None of his friends could have survived outside the military and had chosen the U.S. Army as a career by default.

A crew manning a two ton truck full of ammunition for the big guns was also waiting for Long. They were heading north to C Battery. Three men were transporting the load. Two were riding in the cab.

Another guard was lying on top of the ammo in the bed of the truck, where an M60 machine gun was positioned on the roof. He explained that he was actually a personnel clerk from the base camp supporting operations. Until today he had never left the safe confines of the headquarters unit. With only two weeks left in Vietnam, he had decided to volunteer to serve as guard for one of these daily ammo runs to and from H.Q. He didn't want to return home and tell his family and friends that he'd remained on a large base his entire tour of duty.

His name was James, a friendly and outgoing black man around 20 years old. He couldn't stop talking excitedly about returning home in two weeks. He told them that he was from Cleveland and couldn't wait to see his family and start college.

He was ecstatic about getting a new red Ford Mustang convertible, for which he had been saving the past year. The new recruits were envious but listened to how happy he was about returning home to freedom from the military grind.

Then James explained. "The only reason this ammo truck is stopping here is because we were ordered to pick up something from the first sergeant. He wants it delivered to one of his lifer buddies in C Battery."

"What is it?" Tim asked.

"It turns out to be only a couple cases of beer. As soon as we get that additional cargo we're heading north," James said.

The green soldiers shot the breeze with James until Long showed up twenty minutes later. It was now 0800. After the perfunctory meeting they headed to the mess tent.

"I don't know about you guys but I like the section I was assigned to," Tim said. They found an empty spot on the ground where they could sit as a group. The meal would be one of the few occasions for them to be together. In less than twenty-four hours they had already begun to establish their own lives in the unit.

Tim laughed. "I was up late getting high and listening to great soul music with some brothers. This place ain't half as bad as I expected. No, sir!"

"Yeah, it's better than I expected too," Bill added. "Dan and I were assigned to the fire directional center. I stayed up late talking with the other guys in our section. They're from all over the States."

"What about you, Dan?" Tim asked.

"I listened to some of their conversation but most of the time I spent reading."

"What the hell are you doing reading, boy?" Bobby asked, shaking his head. "The guys I'm with are okay too, I guess. The only thing is that I got stuck with a fucking Chink for a section chief. I'll guess I'll have to learn to live with it."

"You're going to have to forget about racial prejudice over here. We're in this together whether you like it or not," Dan said, taken aback.

"That may be, but it's not going to change how I feel or how I was raised. Some things you can't change. Frankly, I don't want to," Bobby said. He jumped up and left pissed.

Dan and Bill were stunned. Tim broke the silence. "Don't worry about it. I'm used to that fucking shit. It doesn't bother me. Fuck no." He smiled, stood, and said: "I have to go now. See you guys around."

"I don't understand. I thought all that would have been left behind," Bill said naively.

"Not with people like Bobby," Dan said. "He was born a good ole boy and he's going to die one. We better go to our bunker and unpack since we have to pull duty after all. I'm scheduled for this afternoon, and I believe that you're scheduled for tonight." They stood up and left the mess tent.

The ammo truck unexpectedly returned. It had been gone a little over a half hour. The driver jumped out and began frantically looking for the First Sergeant. Bill walked over.

"You returned so soon. What's up?" he asked.

"Fucking Charlie sniper shot our guard in the head," the driver yelled. "He was riding on top. Hell, he didn't even know what hit him. We radioed and had a helicopter fly him to a hospital but it was too late. We need another guard so we can finish the ammo run. You know where the fuck the first sergeant is?"

They both nodded no. The driver ran off.

Dan could see that Bill was shocked and almost in tears and tried to console him. "In the past two days we've seen both a Vietnamese and an American killed. Neither one of their deaths makes any sense. These are not the heroic casualties of war one normally thinks about happening. Yet I'm sure that their families won't miss them any less. It appears this place truly is one big combat zone. Who knows what tomorrow will bring?"

Bill tried to explain. "Yeah, I know, and James was… What bothers me is it was something he didn't have to do. Think about his family. I remember how we received the news about Chris' death. He was my next-door neighbor and closest childhood friend. He was the bravest person I've ever met. I hope I don't put our families through the same anguish all over again."

They walked away in silence.

~ ~ ~ ~ ~

They immediately became absorbed in their new jobs. They kept busy to avoid thinking about home. With each passing day they realized how wonderful it had been to be with their family and friends.

They shielded themselves against the devastation of Vietnam. In conversation they embellished the reality of their experiences at home.

It was the dry season in Vietnam. Rain was not something they had to contend with yet but the dust was worse. It was everywhere. No one was completely clean in Vietnam. The water smelled as if it was funneled directly from the waste of a chemical factory. Other GIs purified the water for them. To be safe, they added too many chemicals to kill the jungle bacteria. At times the water was so repulsive that it was useless to wash with and impossible to drink.

The tropical dirt and grime penetrated a quarter inch below the surface of the skin. To get clean, the men had to wipe their bodies with soapy rags until clean sweat began to flow freely.

~ ~ ~ ~ ~

At 2000 hours a few men congregated in the back room of the fire directional command bunker to gulp down the free army issue beer and soda.

When the new recruits were present, the seasoned troops told war stories to scare the living fucking hell out of them.

Caldwell, Flower Power, Bill and Dan were drinking warm beer and reminiscing about home. 'Where Have All The Flowers Gone?' by Peter, Paul and Mary was playing over a tape deck in the dimly lit room.

"I brought a few joints to toke on. Anybody bring some pills to pop?" one soldier asked.

"Yeah, I got some here," a second said. He passed the assortment to the first soldier, who threw them down his throat without any caution.

"Well, how's our new recruits doing?" Caldwell asked.

"Okay, I guess," Bobby answered. "There isn't as much action as I expected."

"Oh, don't worry, it will happen soon enough," Flower Power said. "Then you'll wish the fuck it never had.

Remember there's no front line here, so sometimes it's hot and sometime it's cold."

A smoking joint was passed around. Flower Power inhaled deeply and sent it on to Bill, who nonchalantly handed it to Dan. He refused it and quickly left the room. Bill passed it to Caldwell, who inhaled immediately.

"That fucking goody-two-shoes thinks he's better than the rest of us. He'll have to face the reality of this fucking hole," Caldwell said. He inhaled deeply and held his breath. Then he exhaled and continued. "I don't think he'll ever be one of us. I say fuck Pencil Neck! That's all right. He'll get his one day."

"That's a good name for him—Pencil Neck," one soldier laughed. "Wait till that bastard needs one of us when things get hot. He'll see that all that crap that he's hanging on to has no place here. The most we can do is survive, even though all of us become lowlife scum-bags in the process."

"I think he's okay. He's just different. Dan is one of the few men enlisted men here who has a college education," Bill said hesitantly,

"Different is okay," Caldwell said. "It's just that that mother fucker is not going to make it the way he is." He stared at him with hate in his eyes. Bill was speechless.

Bill thought, "It will be a long time before I can hold my own against these combat worn soldiers."

He finished his beer and tossed it on the ground.

"Hey man, can't you read the sign?" Flower Power interrupted.

They looked up at the graffiti above the doorway.

THIS is your rat exit - Keep it clean

"You know, everywhere I've been in this country I've seen graffiti," Bill said. "It's amazing how much it says most of the time."

"I remember the first graffiti I ever saw in Vietnam," Flower Power said. "It was in a barracks at Cam Ranh Bay. It said,

What if they called a war and nobody came?

Shit, man, I've been thinking about that ever since I arrived at this godforsaken place."

Abruptly Caldwell stood up. "I've got an idea. I've got a brilliant fucking idea! Let's paint one of the walls white in our party room. We can write anything on it that we want!"

"Do it tonight," Flower Power agreed. "But we ought to name it something."

"We'll get the name later. First, anybody know where we can locate some white paint?" Caldwell asked.

"I'll get it," one of the stoned soldiers said. When he returned, they removed every obstacle in front of the nondescript blank plywood wall.

"Aw, I think this is fucking crazy," said the soldier with the paint. "Let's forget about it."

"Bitch, bitch, bitch, that's all you do is fucking bitch," Caldwell argued.

"The project is a joke but it has a purpose. This is a creative project of love which fills our intrinsic need for self-expression!" Flower Power, very high, exclaimed.

"It just is what it is," Caldwell responded to his hippie counterpart.

The blank wall was painted white in less than an hour.

Then everyone stared at it not knowing where or how to begin.

Over the tape deck played 'Piece of My Heart' by Janis Joplin from her album *Big Brother and the Holding Company*.

Flower Power jumped up and yelled, "That's it! That's it! Give me a paintbrush. The artist will begin. Stand aside please!"

The psychedelic artist took a paintbrush and painted the title on the wall.

Caldwell was mystified as he watched the maestro. When he was through, Flower Power stood waiting for their approval. They stared at the wall and were stumped. No one had any idea of why he was so proud of his creation.

Finally Caldwell spoke. "I don't get it, what the fuck does it mean?"

"Simple," Flower Power explained. "All of us are nothing but a bunch of faggots over here. All of us have gone crazy one way or another. This place is abnormal, and it's impossible for us to remain normal. The longer we're here the more we realize it. I mean it isn't just because we're involved in war. It's a crazy fucked up war that we aren't even trying to win, let alone question the whole morality of this war or any war."

Caldwell shook his head in disgust. "I just wanted to do it because I thought it would be fun. Let's not philosophize too much or you're going to fucking ruin it for all of us."

"Besides, I don't think I'm any crazier than I was before I came to Nam," one soldier said. "It's just that I realize how crazy I am now and couldn't give a flying fuck either."

Flower Power was revved up. "That makes it even better! The only difference between people back home in dreamland and us is that we know we're faggots. We all know we're all fucked up."

A soldier stood up. "Give me a black magic marker. I have an idea." He wrote this immediately under the title:

Relieve Your Innertension — Write on the Wall

After he was through he turned to them, saying, "What do ya think? I think this is what Flower Power is trying to say."

"Now that makes a helluva lot more sense to me," Caldwell said. "I know exactly what I'm going to paint on the wall! I'm going to paint a beautiful babe in a tiny fucking yellow bikini with red polka dots."

The soldiers approached the wall and chose blank spaces to scrawl their first utterances on the Bitch Wall.

"Everyone has to put something on the wall before they leave tonight. There's only one rule—no one can criticize what anyone else puts on the wall!" yelled Flower Power.

An explosion of creative energy ignited. Some thoughts reverberated from their despair-ridden souls, while others displayed their indomitable spirit. The wall became the unifying force within the unit. They carried it in their hearts.

These thoughts evolved on the wall.

When they were finished with the wall that evening, it looked like this:

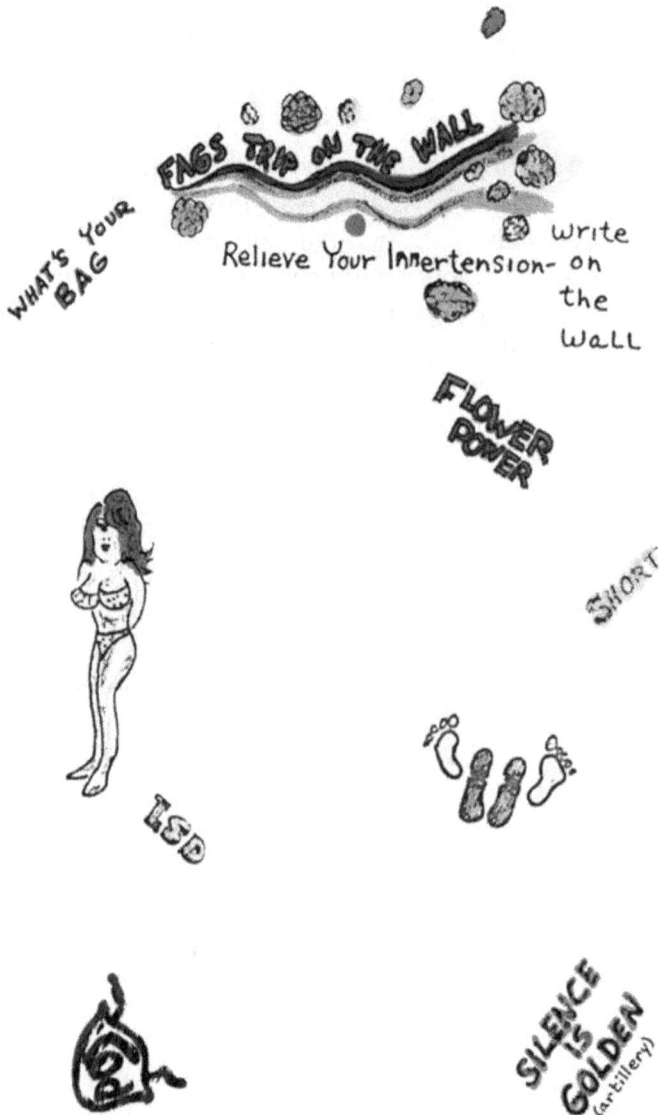

Each time they returned to LZ Lady, they scrambled to the Bitch Wall to tell their stories. The wall would continue to evolve even when they were not stationed at A Battery basecamp. The war graffiti would reveal what burned deeply within their souls.

As it told each man's personal history in a way that nothing else could, the men of the unit became more drawn to it. They felt compelled to visit it nightly, to see what story or joke or drawing had been added that day.

They communicated their most personal thoughts, which they would never have had the courage to verbalize. The wall held the thoughts of all those who had become weak, vulnerable and crazy since arriving in Vietnam.

Many times they would not say a word to each other, listening intensely to the 60's protest music and getting wasted. But the once blank canvas openly wept and shouted for joy on their behalf.

The Beat Goes On

Chapter 4: ONE MONTH LATER

BOBBY WAS PSYCHOLOGICALLY PREPARED to become engaged in the glory of combat long before Vietnam. He knew that his father would be proud of him, and he was determined to relive his father's acclaim as a war hero. He was enjoying life at the gun section much more than he had anticipated and did not understand why the other men in the unit did not share his gung-ho attitude. To the core, Bobby was a hawk, but it bothered him that the Army would not allow the other men to fight the war to win. If allowed, he thought they could stomp the Vietcong's ass in no time. Then again, he figured, "fuck it" and he didn't allow himself to think about anything except combat, sex, and free beer.

Tim became enmeshed in a hedonistic hybrid of the Black culture that was solely indigenous to Vietnam. They spoke their own language. More than back home, there was pride in their private lingo, since it brought the familiar into a combat setting. But Tim never stopped thinking about Annie. His love for her and his children remained his tenuous lifeline to reality.

Meanwhile Dan had alienated himself from the other men in FDC. He seldom spoke except when Bill would strain himself to make conversation with him. Vietnam was becoming even worse for Dan. He clung more passionately to his inner intellectual journey. For the first time he had no idea where this introspective expedition would lead. But it made no rational difference to him. He kept contemplating— more Nietzsche, more Sartre, more Camus.

Bill's boyhood naiveté kept him almost untouched by fear so far. He was the only one of the four who continued to make any effort to talk with the others. Bill regarded friends highly and always made the first effort to remain in contact. Because they had arrived at A Battery together, in his heart he believed they had a special bond. But to the others it was a vague bond, a simple matter of happenstance. Bill knew what it meant to lose a best friend in Vietnam. He thought about his friend Chris all the time. He knew that the same thing could happen again.

The unit met the Vietcong a few times in minor skirmishes—snipers, grenades, sappers sneaking into the camp with explosives. But the prospect of heavy combat hung over their heads. No one knew what would happen.

~ ~ ~ ~ ~

It soon became obvious who were the elite in Vietnam. It was not the officers or the high-ranking NCOs. Many times it was a private. The elite were the short-timers, the men who had less than thirty days left in a unit. Bobby was the first to come abruptly into contact with this reality in his gun section. He was assisting two other men in giving a tune-up to the engine for their section's eight-inch artillery piece. Charlie Johnson had six months left in country while Tommy Shraft had exactly two weeks left before he returned home.

"I don't know what the hell is wrong with this motor," complained Shraft. "Ah! I don't really give a flying fuck anyway! I'm getting too short to worry about this shit."

Then nose-to-nose to Bobby he gloated, "Two more weeks, Swenson. Two weeks! Eat your fucking heart out." Jeering at Bobby, he laughed, got his gear, and went to lunch.

THERE ARE NO BONES IN ICE CREAM

FLIPPER IS A FISH

If a guy has one more strip than you —— Forget it.

"SHORT! You're sorry Charlie!" he yelled, throwing back his head and strutting off. They stared at him enviously.

"Let's see, maybe this will fix the problem," said Charlie abruptly. "Start it up, Bobby, it should run now." The engine started immediately. They were both elated. "Let's go to lunch now. Let's didi mow the area!"

"Didi mow" is Vietnamese for "let's get the hell out of here."

~ ~ ~ ~ ~

On the same day Bill received unexpected news. He was told to go to the orderly room and meet with First Sergeant Long.

Long was in his late forties or early fifties, bald except for the thinning carrot-colored hair on the sides of his head, and had skin so white that he looked like an albino. His body was thickly covered with the same bright red hair. The first sergeant was around 5' 10" with a huge potbelly that was accentuated by his exceptionally skinny arms and legs. He loved walking around without a shirt and flaunting his huge belly that was directly related to the amount of Budweiser he consumed daily.

First Sergeant Long was not your typical Army lifer. He would return to the United States much richer than when he arrived in Vietnam. He sold a large portion of the supplies issued to the unit to the South Vietnamese Army or on the black market. Some of the supplies ended up in the hands of the enemy since the first sergeant was not really sure to whom he was selling.

Fortunately, supplies were in overabundance so the unit would always get enough provisions eventually, but not always as promptly. You did not have to be slick to get away with this sort of minor corruption. No one really cared.

At the same time, Long was a good leader despite his major problems. For example, he was prejudiced against the blacks. Everyone was aware of it but no one complained because he was basically fair to all the men. He was uneducated and probably would not have done well as a civilian. He would most likely have continued raising hell, but without ever amounting to anything. Somehow, as a career soldier, he rose to a prestigious rank. It was undeniable that his greatest asset was that it was impossible not to like him.

As Bill walked into the orderly room, he could not figure out why he been ordered to meet with Long after breakfast. The company clerk was sitting at his field desk, a trunk painted army green that unfolded into a desk.

"Is Long here? I've been requested to meet with him," Bill said hesitantly.

"I'll get him for you," the company clerk said and left for the first sergeant's tent. When he returned a few minutes later he said, "He'll be with you in a couple minutes."

Bill said thanks and waited for Long. When he finally arrived at the orderly room tent, it was obvious that Long had just awakened. He was hung over and bare-chested. As soon as Long shook his hand, Bill could smell the pungent stale beer and cigarette smoke on his breath.

The first sergeant asked, "I suppose you're wondering why I called you to my office?" Bill nodded. "I heard some good things about you. Would you be interested in being my company clerk?"

Bill wasn't sure what to say since he had heard that you had to close your eyes to Long's outrageous behavior. He asked, "How soon do you need to know?"

"I need to know by tomorrow morning after breakfast. I'm not surprised you have to think about it. I'm sure that you're just getting to know the men in the FDC. However, remember that this is one of the best jobs in the battery since you don't have to pull guard duty or any other extra duty. You're only responsible to fulfilling duties that relate directly to Captain Biddle and me. You're welcome to discuss it with my current company clerk. He's a short timer. It's a damn good thing too since he isn't worth a shit."

The company clerk was unfazed. He was used to Long's comments.

"Well, what do you think?" Long smiled and looked directly into Bill's eyes.

Bill replied politely. "It's just that this is something I hadn't anticipated. I appreciate that you've asked me. And you're right, it would be great not to have to pull extra duty of any kind. I'll let you know tomorrow morning after breakfast as instructed. Thank you for asking me." They shook hands again.

Walking back to the FDC bunker, Bill thought about what it would be like to work for Captain Biddle and Long. He had been impressed with the captain from the beginning.

Captain Biddle was the chief officer in the unit and a West Point graduate. Everyone admired him. Although he was not anything like First Sergeant Long, the captain chose to ignore Long's questionable activities. He was 6' 2" and in his early thirties. He was tall, slender and handsome with thick blonde hair and blue eyes. Most of the day he was reading, interacting with the other officers, or thoroughly inspecting everything in the unit to insure his men's safety. He was not always as open with the enlisted men, but they knew he treated them with respect and an unusual kindness that they did not receive from most of the officers.

The captain was a gentleman, who was drawn to the military service out of a deep sense of patriotism which stemmed from his conservative Midwestern background. He saw himself caught in a police action that he had not entirely come to terms with on three counts.

First, the reasons the United States was involved in Vietnam seemed nebulous to him at best. Second, there was an underlying war between the lifers and the drafted men. The peace movement back home affected many of the soldiers who were drafted. This had had an unsettling effect on the general morale of the men in A Battery. Third, and even more disconcerting, the military was not allowed to fight this conflict to win, and he wondered how much longer it could continue.

He was compelled to keep this entirely to himself and pretend not to see the hypocrisy of the situation. His only consolation was that he was stationed in Vietnam for only one year and then would return home to his wife and children.

Bill took all this under careful consideration before deciding to work as company clerk. However, even more important to him was that he related to his comrades in the unit. He would miss working with the men in the FDC. Being clerk was exceptionally demanding, allowed for little free time during the day, and often required overtime.

Bill was naive as to why he'd been asked, but he had already proven himself capable in the FDC. He presented an excellent appearance that the clerk's position required as first point of contact for the unit. The combination of his attractive physical appearance and good sense of humor, even in times of stress, made him popular with everyone. It also helped that he had some college education and was exceptionally bright.

The next morning Bill met with Long to accept the position. The first sergeant seemed genuinely happy with his decision. Immediately after his meeting with Long, he ran to the FDC sleeping bunker to tell Dan. As usual, Bill found him reading.

"I've decided to take the job as company clerk," Bill said.

"What? I thought you'd decided not to take it." Dan was caught off-guard.

"Yeah, I know. I talked to the guy who's clerk now and he seems to enjoy the job. Dan, I'll have regular hours. It will be like an ordinary desk job. Except that my desk will be an Army trunk."

"What about all your talk about not wanting to leave the guys where we've been assigned?" Dan scolded him.

"Oh, I know what I said. But after I really thought about it I realized that it's too good to turn down," Bill responded, laughing. "Oh yes, I found out that I have to move closer to the orderly room. But don't worry about it. I'll still see you guys all the time."

"It won't be the same without you. It certainly won't be as lively. Besides, you're the only person that I can talk to here," Dan said almost sadly.

"Thanks, Dan. I better go tell the other guys." He paused. "I think they're okay, Dan. You just don't give them a chance," Bill said.

Love

"I beg to differ with you on that issue," Dan interrupted condescendingly.

"You cut yourself off from them. You spend all your spare time reading. It's no wonder they don't understand you."

"I'm keeping it that way too! In fact, after you're gone, I'll probably spend even more time in bunk. Look at them. They're either running to the whorehouse or getting wasted. They have to keep running so they don't have to stop and face themselves."

"What?" asked Bill, only half understanding.

"You really don't get it, do you?"

"I guess not," Bill admitted.

"Their behavior is pitiful and disgusting because they're trying to fill their emptiness inside through external means. It doesn't work! It never did," explained Dan, nearly yelling. "Yet they continue to try to fill the void inside with trinkets and touchdowns." He stood and became more intense. "In their words, if it isn't the whorehouse, it's pot, it's booze or it's popping pills. Running, running, running, that's all they're doing."

"Surely you don't think any of us are any different?" Bill asked. "Even you run in your own way. You're always running to your books. Besides, I don't think sex is the worst trap a person can fall into over here."

"You may be right," Dan answered. "Besides, at least my escape leads to some positive growth. I've learned to accept the onslaught. There's nothing we can do to stop it."

"I guess you're right. But I still don't think they're all that bad," Bill added.

"Don't you think you ought to tell the others you're leaving?" Dan asked curtly as he went abruptly back to reading his book. Dan knew that Bill looked up to him and relied on him for support. So he cut off their conversation and remained silent to aggravate his only friend in the unit.

"Yeah, I guess you're right. See you later." Responding to Dan's aloofness, he looked back and stood there until Dan looked at him. Bill said good-bye to him. Dan smiled and waved him away. He ran out of the bunker to tell the others about his decision.

"He's a real man!.. no where" The Beattles

After Bill left, Dan thought, "If Bill had not taken the job, the opportunity could have been mine. I have my college education. I could have had the luxury of just keeping to myself at that desk job.

"My decision not to go to Officers Candidate School was a wise move. These ninety-day wonders are a joke. They really are shake and bake officers. It's good I didn't commit to the military longer. It's the only thing worse than being clumped with the enlisted men. I don't care if I'm out of my element."

Pencil Neck

But their conversation had forced Dan to question how he was going to survive. "It's beneath me to play their superficial games and pretend I'm one of them. Maybe Bill is right. Maybe the other men are not all that bad. But befriending them would mean giving in to their depravity. At all costs I must hold on to the values I brought here to Vietnam. But if my internal struggle has manifested itself in my relationships with the other men, it's evolved into a no-win for me. The two distinct sides are a line in the sand— depravity or isolation."

Character is what you stand for, Reputation is what you fall for.

~ ~ ~ ~ ~

Tim was enjoying commo section more than ever. He was likable, easy-going, and everyone accepted him on his arrival. He was enjoying the routine of sex, drugs and rock-and-roll.

He was happier and freer in Vietnam than back home, since he was without social pressures of overt racial prejudice. People kept their disdain hidden from the blacks.

Tim knew it was just in case they needed their white asses saved during combat. But most of the time he felt that this unspoken truce was an even tradeoff. Tim was keenly aware that he would return home to face the same hate he had left behind.

He enjoyed listening to the seasoned vets in his section. One day in the late afternoon, Tim was taking a break with the men in his barracks. They were smoking some weed, listening to Motown music, reminiscing about home, and discussing how they spent their paychecks on every sensual pleasure available to the American GI's in Vietnam.

"How can you afford it? Most of my money is sent home to my family," Tim asked.

"Oh that! Well, I just keep all my monies to myself. You see my wife works, and I figure that she can take care of herself," a soldier interjected, speaking through a drugged stupor.

Another replied to Tim, "Man, you must be a fucking idiot! You'll soon understand that over here half the men keep more of their paycheck than their wives know about. We have to have money to do things here to release our tension or we'll go crazy!"

"I couldn't do that," said Tim defiantly. But he thought to himself, "Or could I? Everyone else seems to think it's okay. Maybe I need to consider their suggestion seriously."

Vietnam is a bummer.

Suddenly Lowe barged into the bunker. He was returning a week late from his R&R in Australia. Everyone had been wondering what had happened to the wild man of the unit. He returned on the helicopter that had just dropped off some supplies to the unit. Lowe usually had a story to embellish about a girl at one of the houses. But on second look it appeared that he was having difficulty in walking and was in a great deal of pain.

"What the hell you walking so fucking goofy for?" asked a soldier.

"This is what I get for having the best fuck of my life," said Lowe.

"Man, I've had some wild fucks," said a second soldier. "But not one that I couldn't hardly walk the next day." Everyone laughed.

In spite of himself Lowe started laughing too. But with each laugh his pain got worse. "You mother fuckers are killing me. Now shut the fuck up and I'll tell you what happened to the man."

He continued, "I met this beautiful woman and we fell in love. Her name was Mona. She had long blonde hair, blue eyes and the most beautiful long legs you have ever seen. She had the kind of legs that you can't wait to get wrapped around your waist so you can fuck her to the max. Wow! She was the first white woman I'd ever fucked." All of a sudden everyone was quiet and listening intently.

Lowe was delighted to have their full attention. He stood and became animated, gesturing.

"We were together my last three days in Sydney. On our last night we got drunk and decided that we'd go for a romantic walk on the beach because we'd fallen in love."

He paused and smiled to himself.

"We started getting romantic. We found ourselves naked lying on the sand. Hell, we began fucking by the moonlight on the beach. Because we were both so drunk, neither one of us noticed that sand had slipped inside her. Anyway it was like we were getting rubbed with sandpaper. We fell asleep in each other's arms. It was wonderful. Then when we woke up in the morning neither one of us could walk. All we could do was lie on the beach in pain. The lifeguards had to have the ambulance take us to the hospital. I've never been in so much fucking pain in my life."

Everyone laughed uncontrollably and, in spite of himself, so did Lowe. Through extreme discomfort he said, "You lousy mother fuckers, you could at least have some respect for a man who's still in pain. If you don't believe it, I'll show you."

He unzipped his pants and pulled out his penis.

The first soldier yelled through his laughter, "It's been through a fucking meat grinder."

Everyone laughed again non-stop. There was no pity for the man who had just returned from Australia and had the best fuck in his life.

You've Damned
If You Do.
Damned If You Don't.
I'd Rather Be
Damned for
Doing Nothing.

?

FAG

To Be Fat is cool
I am cool
Real cool
Extra Cool

"On the whole, I'd rather be in Philadelphia."
W. C. Fields

Chapter 5: NIGHT IN NAM

SECOND LIEUTENANT BUCHANAN was despised by most of the men for his arrogance towards the enlisted men. Buchanan was twenty years old and the stereotypical "shake-and-bake" officer. Because there was a shortage of officers, the Army began recruiting from college campuses. Buchanan had been in school for a just a year before signing up.

After only three months in Officer Candidate School, he was appointed a second lieutenant. In almost every case, a 90-day wonder second lieutenant was not the same caliber of officer as a West Point graduate. Buchanan enjoyed flaunting his rank daily to everyone. He didn't realize what most of the enlisted men said about him behind his back, or that if he was not careful, he might receive an unpleasant surprise from one of them.

It was not unusual for the enlisted men to teach a lesson to someone if he was not playing by the rules in Vietnam, no matter how corrupt the rules were. For example, he might find an unarmed claymore lying in front of his bunk with his name on it. Usually this sobered young OCS officers to the conformity in Vietnam.

In the command center of FDC there was no discussion taking place. The only sound was from the tape recorder. 'White Rabbit' by Jefferson Airplane from the album *Surrealistic Pillow* was blasting away.

Suddenly over the radio a message rang from Headquarters Unit: "Fire mission!"

Caldwell ran over to the tape recorder and shut it off. The siren blasted with three long cranks. Gun sections 1 and 3 were called up. The other men in the bunker got in their combat positions.

Buchanan was the officer in charge that night. He received the orders for the firing mission and went to the panoramic telescope to aim the big guns dead center on target. With well-practiced precision the men in FDC moved to their assigned positions and executed the mission flawlessly. In less than five minutes the target on the hills to the north ignited with explosions of dozens of shells. Bobby at Gun Section 1 could see the hills smoldering from the artillery impacts.

"End of mission. Right on target. Good going, men!" said a voice over the radio in the command bunker to the directional team.

Caldwell responded on the radio with a thicker Bronx accent than usual. "Roger-over-and-out." He turned to the men in the FDC command bunker. With his hands on his waist, stomach out of his shirt, satisfied, he said, "What did they expect? We're A Battery. We're the best!"

Then over the telephones to the men in the gun sections he relayed, "End of mission. Right on target—thanks to your fantastic FDC!"

After the mission the men in FDC went back to what they were doing before. Once again there was no conversation. The bored silence resumed. The tape recorder was flicked back on and 'Plastic Fantastic Lover' by Jefferson Airplane was on maximum volume.

~ ~ ~ ~ ~

In Gun Section #1, Bobby was unconcerned as he checked the unused powder charges from the previous firing mission. "Hey, guess what? I used charge 4's on the fire mission instead of charge 5's!"

Sergeant Chen stood up and threw his helmet. "Are you fucking crazy? They said we hit right on target."

"Oh, to that we owe our thanks to our fantastic FDC," Bobby said in Caldwell's Brooklyn accent, mocking his arrogance on the telephone. Everyone laughed except for Sergeant Chen.

"Man, it's over. We ain't got time to hassle ourselves over some shit like that," said one soldier as he got a joint from his pocket.

"Yeah, man. Cut-dat-honky-bo-jive!" said another. "Pass-me-dat-stuff-man." He puffed the joint and hit Chen on the shoulder. "We got 'em! Smoked their hole!"

Then he gave Chen the joint. Chen inhaled and passed it. He held his breath with the smoke deep in his lungs.

As Chen let out the smoke, he gave a sigh and said, "Where were we? Oh yeah, we were all cruising around McDonald's with our women."

They all laughed and concurred, continuing their interrupted discussion about an imaginary night out on the town back home.

Chevrolet sucks-up all competition

GTO = NO. 1

Pussy Cars

Corvette
Comet
Cobra
442
RR
GTX
RT

No. 2

GTO's Blow-off

~ ~ ~ ~ ~

Tim, Bill and another soldier were pulling duty together at Outpost #1.

"How come you, the company clerk, has to pull guard duty?" asked Edmonds. "I never thought the First Sergeant would pull something like this. He never did it to the other clerk."

THE ARMY IS EXACTLY what WE ARE FIGHTING— Communism

"Well, nine men are on sick leave or injured, eight just left for home, plus we haven't received any replacements for a while," explained Bill. "Since we're so short of men, I have to pull guard duty for the next couple of weeks."

"Shit, man, that's not fair. The First Sergeant is always at the whorehouse. You know you won't be able to sleep in the morning like the rest of us!" said Tim, flipping his helmet down in front of his face. "You're fucked, desk boy."

~ ~ ~ ~ ~

In the mess tent Buck Owens was singing 'I've Got A Tiger By The Tail.' Two NCO's, both lifers, were sitting around a table laughing and drinking beer.

If you don't look to the future, you will have no future in the army.

"Did you hear about the first sergeant?" asked one lifer.
"No, what happened to that old S.O.B. this time?"

"Well, today he and the medic went out on a pussy run. And they got drunk and laid," laughed the first lifer, to the bewilderment of the other man. "Well, First Sergeant Long and the medic were late getting back to camp so Long told the medic to step on it. They were busting ass down the road and a gook cart pulls out in front of their jeep. So the medic tries to avoid hitting the cart and he pulls off onto the shoulder of the road. They hit a rock and the jeep turns upside down in a fucking wet rice paddy."

Both the lifers laughed hysterically. "Listen, listen. Someone said that the first sergeant thought he was drowning in the paddy and came up fighting for air!" He demonstrated by waving his hands wildly in the air. They both continued laughing and took another drink of warm beer.

"Are they both all right?" asked the second lifer, trying to calm himself down.

"Oh yeah, the medic is okay, but the first sergeant got a crick in his back. He can't even stand up straight, much less visit his slant-eyed girl for weeks." They laughed again. "Guess what else? Then he put his clerk on guard duty!"

"Bill Freeze?" asked the second lifer.

"Yeah. Well, the first sergeant walked into the orderly room like this." He demonstrated Long's new hunched-over walk. "And you know Bill, he busted his ass laughing at him. Long was pissed! Well, later on the first sergeant told Bill Freeze they were short of men so he would have to take a turn and pitch in at pulling guard duty." Both lifers laughed more.

"That's nothing," continued the next lifer. "You shoulda seen Long trying to salute the captain!" He demonstrated again, pulling his right arm up to salute with his left. They laughed uncontrollably again when the first sergeant entered the mess tent. "What the hell's going on here?" he yelled. He was hunched over in pain, carrying an ice pack over his buttocks with his good arm.

"Oh, nothing. I was getting all of us another beer," said the first lifer. "Ya want one?"

"Did you ever know me to turn one down? Start that song over again," First Sergeant Long said gruffly.

As a private sitting, reading a magazine, and smoking near the tape deck started the same record again, the second lifer asked, "Why are you being so rough on Bill Freeze? He's a good man."

"Well, when we were at Bong Son, I fell asleep one afternoon with the flaps up on my tent. When I fell asleep, the sun was on the opposite side of the tent, but it moved to the other side of the tent and burnt the fucking shit out of my belly, neck and arms," explained Long.

"Yeah, but why did..." started the first lifer.

"Wait just a fuck'n minute and I'll explain," interrupted Long as he took a drink of his beer. "I knew damn good and well Bill knew I would get burnt. That's why he didn't pull the flaps down. So I knew that I'd get even with that son-of-a-bitch some day!" The three lifers laughed triumphantly because they had made hell for the GIs again.

This must be a Lifer.

~ ~ ~ ~ ~

The men gathering in the FDC bunker were high and adding their thoughts to the wall.

By-the-Book Buchanan, Caldwell, and Dan Semple were sitting in the FDC command bunker. Everyone was still listening to music. Flower Power entered.

Buchanan said arrogantly to Flower Power, "What are you doing here? You're not supposed to be on duty for another 24 hours!"

"Peace!" said Flower Power, giving the symbol.

"We don't have room for any of that over here," said Buchanan sarcastically.

"Cool it, man, I'm not in the mood to get into it with you again tonight," answered Flower Power defiantly as he sat down, lit a joint, inhaled, and passed it to the others. As usual, everyone took a toke but Dan.

Buchanan said to Dan, holding in his toke of smoke, "Why don't you at least try some of the evil weed? It might loosen you up, and boy, you need some fucking loosening up!"

"I don't see why I should," said Semple indignantly. "I'm fine the way I am."

"Yeah, you might become one of us," said Flower Power.

"No thanks," answered Dan condescendingly.

Caldwell got fired up after listening to the exchange and yelled, "Pencil Neck, damn it, I ought to beat your fucking face in."

"Lighten up," said Flower Power, waving his head back and forth. "Shine it on."

"We can't force him. Wait until he's in some heavy combat. I don't know, but he's been able to dodge heavy combat since he's been here. Maybe you're our good luck charm, Pencil Neck," said Buchanan.

"That's right," agreed Caldwell. "Remember you can't beat the system over here. So why try? Pencil Neck, just go along with it and make it easier on yourself."

Attempting to reach out in the only way he knew how, Dan said, "No system is better than the people who are in it. Corrupt people necessarily result in a corrupt system. Even good people or mediocre people, like most of us are, need a good system to keep their integrity."

Flower Power, inhaling, said, "That's one of the problems with the army. Over here a corrupt system evolved, or at least it has its bad points. Perhaps building and maintaining a perfect system like a family, a church, a college or a government is impossible. So the utmost of flexibility should be maintained. We just got to be free."

"I think that in any so-called Christian system that's the ideal to be maintained," agreed Dan. "That is, dealing with events and circumstances with wisdom and certain other principles; love, hope, mercy, justice and more. I think studying ethics would be a fascinating subject, don't you, Flower Power?"

"Yeah, I think so too. I don't know whether to chase after the middle class mirage or not when I get back home. I'm not sure I can buy into a system that I believe has lost its flexibility, let alone its values. When I go back, I think I'll grow my hair long and become a hippie. What about you, Caldwell?"

Caldwell, who was unmoved by the whole conversation, retorted, "I'm going to become a New York City policeman, get married, and have some children." Then he took another big toke of marijuana.

"Flower Power," questioned Dan, "then you want to join the movement that's on so many college campuses today? Don't you think you're just following the pack? Today on the college campuses the theatrical elite are creating the drama of Vietnam by occupying school administration buildings across America."

Flower Power responded forcefully. "Do you disagree with the student movement? You think they're wrong or something? Dan, I don't see how any thinking man can, dig me? In fact, I believe this revolution may be the last shout of humanity! In the world, this is now the last shout against the technological society, which exists because of the military industrial complex. You know I believe Eisenhower was right about what he said."

"It may surprise you," answered Dan, "but I don't. But for different reasons than you just stated. The American legend of success and victory in war is not shared by every other nation in the world today. This ill-gotten fate has dangerously detached America from the universal experience of other nations. All the other great nations, exclusive of the United States, have known the humiliation of defeat. This has continued to promote the conviction that the American Way shall prevail in the end. The suspect theory opens us to the caprice that America is exempt from the forces of history that all other great nations have eventually succumbed to."

Excitedly Flower Power said, "Yeah, and the history of Vietnam has been full of bitterness and humiliation. And here we come to set them free. The brunt of this war is falling on the draftee. Eight out of ten men serving in combat don't wanna be here. It's all such a cruel joke."

Buchanan shouted angrily, "Would both you faggots shut the fuck up? Flower Power, you sound like a burnt-out hippie! All you need is the long hair! You already have the love beads. And, Dan, you just can't intellectualize your way out of this war, when are you gonna learn that?"

"Aw, bitch, bitch, bitch, that's all we do over here," complained Caldwell, disgusted. "That's what the Bitch Wall is for. I don't want to hear any more either. Why don't the both of you go to the back room and write something on it and leave the rest of us alone?"

He lit another joint and passed it around. Over the tape recorder played The Byrds' 'Turn, Turn, Turn.'

A time for giving birth,
a time for dying;
A time for killing,
a time for healing;
A time for tears,
a time for laughter;
A time for hating,
a time for loving
A time for war,
a time for peace . . . (Ecclesiastes)

"I've got a message from headquarters to read to you which you aren't supposed to hear," interrupted Bill. "It reads as follows:

```
SUBJECT:  BOB HOPE CHRISTMAS SHOW

1.  BOB HOPE WILL PRESENT HIS ANNUAL CHRISTMAS
SHOW AT THE PHU CAT AIR FORCE BASE THIS YEAR.
2.  DUE TO STRINGENT SECURITY PRECAUTIONS, THE
DATE AND TIME OF THE SHOW IS NOT BEING
ANNOUNCED, HOWEVER, IT IS BELIEVED THAT THE
SHOW WILL BE HELD BETWEEN 20 AND 23 DECEMBER.
3.  UNITS WILL RECEIVE NO MORE THAN 6 HOURS
NOTICE OF THE TIME OF THE SHOW.
4.  BATTERY COMMANDERS WILL SUBMIT THE FOLLOWING
TO THIS HQ, ATTN: S-1 NOT LATER THAN 19 DEC 68.
    A.  APPROXIMATE NUMBER OF PERSONNEL THAT
CAN BE SENT TO THE SHOW IF IT IS HELD AT A TIME
THAT PERSONNEL WILL BE ABLE TO RETURN TO THEIR
BATTERY FOLLOWING THE SHOW.
    B.  NUMBER OF PERSONNEL THAT CAN BE SENT IF
PERSONNEL WILL BE REQUIRED TO STAY OVER NIGHT AT
SERVICE BATTERY DUE TO TIME AND CURFEW ON HIGHWAY
TRAVEL.
5.  NUMBER OF PERSONNEL THAT CAN BE SENT MUST BE
LEFT OPEN TO CHANGE DUE TO TACTICAL REQUIREMENTS.
```

"Fuck it. None of us can go because we're in the field, and they can't afford to send any of us forward. The only ones that can go are the pussies on the big bases," Bill said.

"They see all the other U.S.O. shows anyway!" yelled Caldwell, pissed.

"Yeah, well, that's the way it goes," answered Bill.

~ ~ ~ ~ ~

In the commo section 'I Am Black and Proud' by James Brown was playing on the tape deck. Lowe was dancing and jiving. Except for Hernandez, everyone was black. All of them were drinking and toking some smoke.

"Don't you ever get tired of that song?" asked Hernandez, shaking his head.

"You crazy, man?" asked Lowe. "Dat's my battle song for when I gets back to de States!"

"Why?" asked Hernandez.

Lowe said angrily. "Why? You got a lot of fucking nerve asking me why. Hell, you're a greasy wetback and me a nigger as far as all these honkies are concerned. You know the only reason they're friends with us here is because they're afraid they'll need our help when things get hot."

Electric EYE

"So what?" said Hernandez.

"So what! What do you mean, so what? If I didn't like you, Hernandez, I'd knock the fuck out of you. Why, over here you're supposed to hate Luke the Gook," Lowe responded, yelling. "And they got their guns aimed at us when we march back stateside.

LUKE THE GOOK

"But man," Lowe continued, "they're just as prejudiced here. Don't kid yourself, boy, 'cause none of these honkies will be our friends back home. Oh, except maybe that pretty Jew-boy Bill Freeze, and he's in worse shape than we are 'cause he's a queer. Yeah only honky queers are our friends back home."

"You don't know that Freeze is queer," argued Hernandez. "He just doesn't go to the whorehouse, that's all. You're fucking crazy, Lowe."

Lowe laughed. "Yeah, I know you think Lowe is crazy, and I know he is too. And it's because he knows this world sucks. Oh, well, end of sermon. You know I may run for Congress one day!" He laughed and continued dancing.

"Yeah!" said Hernandez as he got his gear ready and went to guard duty at Outpost #4.

~ ~ ~ ~ ~

Bill was on the phone. "OP #1 calling FDC!"

"Yeah," answered Caldwell. "What do you want?"

"Incoming rounds on OP #1. Request permission to fire!" Bill asked, frightened.

"Wait one," said Caldwell casually. He got the radio receiver phone and called Headquarters unit. "Foxtrot. Foxtrot this is Bill, over."

"Bill, this Foxtrot, over," responded Caldwell.

"Incoming rounds on Outpost number 1! Sentry requests permission to fire." Bill, his voice more frightened, radioed again.

"Wait one," Caldwell said to Bill.

Bill, who was still dodging bullets, rolled in a ball behind the sandbag outpost and yelled, "What the fuck is taking so long? I'll fire anyway."

Caldwell was delighted to hear Bill so frightened. "You do and you'll get court-martialed! You should have just fired anyway and not called in to ask for permission. It's the policy in Vietnam. You may be firing at other Americans, you stupid son-of-a-bitch, although it's doubtful in this case!"

Over the radio from headquarters unit, "Bill, this is Foxtrot, over."

"Wait one, Bill," said Caldwell again. Then the FDC at Headquarters unit replied, "Foxtrot, this is HQ, over."

"HQ, this is B Battery, over."

"Permission to fire granted," responded a voice from Battalion.

"Over and out." Caldwell radioed to Freeze, "OP #1, permission to fire is granted."

Bill immediately started firing and combed everything in sight from the top to the bottom of the hill. He was going to make sure that whatever was out there couldn't shoot back again. Soon after he started firing the M-50 machine gun, the phone rang. He looked back but decided not to answer. Through a drunken stupor Hernandez, who was also on guard duty but asleep, wondered why Bill was not answering the phone.

Bill continued shooting the M-50 machine gun until the barrel glowed red-hot in the moonless night. Then he felt his job was done and answered the phone. "OP #1."

"This is OP #4!" screamed a voice over the phone. "Do you know what you've been doing, you dumb mother-fucker?"

"Yeah, I've been combing the hill. For gooks!" said Bill.

"Well, every other time you combed the hill, you came too far up. We were dodging bullets from you. Our asses are stuck to the ground like glue!"

"No shit?" said Bill. He broke out laughing. Then the voice from OP#4 burst out laughing uncontrollably too. They hung up.

"You know, he's right. It is pretty funny," he said to Hernandez, who did not respond, being in a drug stupor and oblivious to the heavy machine gun fire. Bill shook him violently screaming, "Hernandez, Hernandez, are you okay?"

Hernandez is Home

Though still groggy, Hernandez looked at the damage Bill had done to their outpost and squeaked, "Oh man, we're going to have to fill some more sandbags!"

They laughed wildly and lit joints.

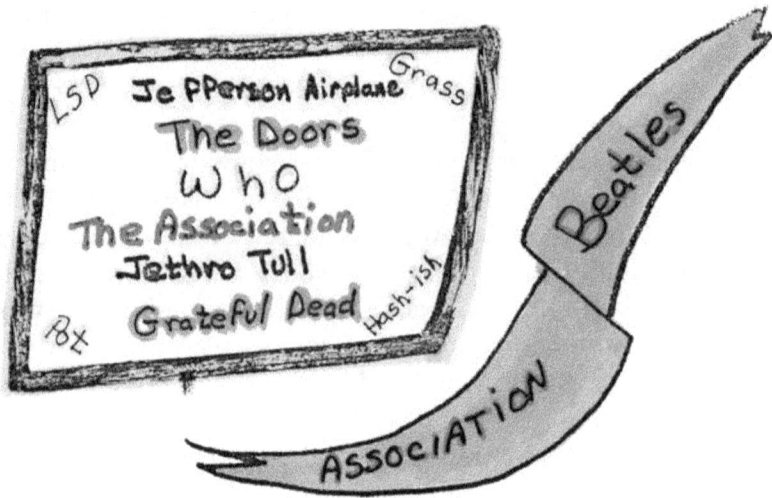

The World is a Kalidascope

With dope there's hope.

Chevrolet sucks up
all competition---
except cars.

Moon

"What are they gonna do,
Send me to Vietnam?

Let THE SPLASH OF COLOR ON THE WALL

Penetrate The Depth of Your Eyes

THEN You Will realize

You're on a trip and having Ball

Chapter 6: COMBAT

IT WAS ALMOST THREE MONTHS since Bobby, Bill, Tim and Dan had been confronted with skirmishes. Several men with them had suffered minor injuries but only three had been airlifted by helicopter out of harm's way. Even the combat worn troops began to think that everything would continue in the near peaceful manner that they were accustomed to enjoying.

In Vietnam there was no front line. It was a guerrilla war, much different from previous wars. In World Wars I and II and in Korea, men could rely on the fact that the ground troops were defending geography to keep the opposition from advancing. But at any moment in Vietnam, heated combat could break out without warning.

On that morning, around 1000 hours one of the men at Observation Post #3 watched enemy troops setting up mortar and rocket artillery on the hill opposite where A Battery was located. Captain Biddle and First Sergeant Long were notified immediately.

At 1020 they came armed with their binoculars to see if this was true. Headquarters and Battalion got a call. Then orders came back to do nothing.

Doing nothing was as anticipated since it was a standing rule in Vietnam that American forces couldn't defend themselves against the enemy, even when they were being attacked, unless they first received permission.

"I'm not gonna get my ass court-martialed for not getting permission to wipe that fucking hill clean of the fucking gooks," Long explained to Captain Biddle as they watched the enemy set up on the hill.

Biddle just stood by and watched the hill. He held the binoculars in his folded arms, knowing as well as the first sergeant that a court-martial came for not following the Army procedures that were created specifically for Vietnam.

"We'll fuck 'em," Long ranted. "I'm already the kill crazy mother fucker they're trying to prevent. Hey, if it looks like a Vietcong… Of course, this could be any Vietnamese since they're all potential enemies. Why don't they just give us the call and we'll take care of these bitches before lunch?"

"Hey, we are ordered not to attack without due provocation. I'd rather keep being captain than get court-martialed," Biddle replied. "They think on that hill there's an elderly woman or child *not* employed by the Vietcong. A young child less than ten years old could be carrying a hand grenade or an elderly woman might be clutching an effective homemade bomb."

"Not surprisingly, they make American soldiers very nervous, especially when I've had friends die or get wounded. And I'm bored," the first sergeant went on.

Under the circumstances, Captain Biddle and Long were powerless. So they sat in their lawn chairs, drank a few beers, and watched the enemy set up their light artillery. In fact the entire unit watched the enemy like the previews of coming attractions for a Saturday matinee movie.

~ ~ ~ ~ ~

It was around 2100 hours and the big guns were firing off excess ammunition. This was an almost daily procedure since there had been too much ammunition produced, some left over from World War II. The different sections took turns performing these missions. Neutral territory was chosen for the firing of the rounds, which sometimes continued for as long as an hour.

That night the routine firing mission ran for around ten minutes. Then Bobby realized that incoming rounds were exploding all over within A Battery's perimeter.

It had been like any other night. Most of the men were asleep or in a drugged stupor. There was no time to warn anyone.

But the Vietcong were not only firing mortar and rockets into the safety of their unit. That was a diversion. Within a few minutes, sappers were around the unit, throwing homemade incendiary grenades, focusing primarily on the personnel bunkers where the soldiers slept. Once one grenade was ignited, the shrapnel saturated the entire area within the confines of a bunker. There was no place to hide.

It was difficult to see the sappers in the dark. But the Vietcong were trained to know exactly where each American soldier was located. They wore only black loincloths and blackened their bodies with paint, grease, soot and dirt. Worse, it was a dark night—cloudy, no moon, no stars. It was almost like being inside a cave with no lights, except when a mortar exploded out of the darkness. This was why the sappers were especially effective tonight. They wanted to kill as many Americans as possible.

Tim was asleep in the commo section bunker. He heard people yelling and instinctively knew that A Battery was under attack. He grabbed his M-16 rifle, ammunition, and gas mask located immediately next to his bunk. There was no time to put on his pants, so he jumped into his boots and struggled to find the exit to the bunker, running out armed in his army issue white briefs. The canvas flap covering the exit flipped open. He could see the lights coming from the flares sent up to light inside the perimeter of A Battery.

"Get your fucking ass on the ground! There's something thrown into our hooch!" he heard.

Tim heard it rolling across the floor. He jumped ten feet and threw his body on the ground as far away as possible. He wondered if he was going to die.

The incendiary grenade exploded. He blacked out from concussion.

Dan was on duty at the FDC command bunker, the safest place in the unit, with guards assigned to protect each entrance. The unit couldn't operate without this area being fully functional.

He listened to the landing of the artillery, gunshots and grenades going off throughout the unit. Frozen, Dan hovered in the corner with his standard Army issue combat paraphernalia—gun, ammo and helmet.

"Am I going to have to shoot this thing at them? Am I going to have to return fire? Am I going to pull the trigger?" Dan was almost totally immobilized by his fear.

But Bobby, firing excess rounds as he stood by the artillery piece in gun section #1, was delighted. Hunched by his gun with his M-16 drawn, he scanned the perimeter for a sapper. He shot up a flare to light the area around Section #1.

That was when he saw a near-naked sapper heading towards the big gun. Bobby was deep in the mud, hidden and watching. He eyed his first opportunity to kill a gook as the sapper approached Bobby and the big gun.

He attached the bayonet to the rifle barrel end and waited for the sapper to get ahead of him. When the sapper passed, Bobby drove the bayonet into the center of his back. Then, as the flare lighted the big gun and stacks of shells, while mortars and guns popped all around him, he stabbed the screaming sapper over and over again to fucking make sure the gook was dead.

As the sun rose, Bobby was a hero. He smiled, walking around the unit, knowing that he would have other opportunities to demonstrate his heroism. He enjoyed killing gooks.

Things were winding down. Mortars no longer crashed and popped. Meanwhile Bill was on guard duty at Observation Post #4. One of the guys began shooting the M-60 machine gun, expertly combing the hill with uniform firing power. Flares were shot in the air so as to detect the slightest movement. Bill grabbed his M-16 rifle, put the ammo cartridge in place and began firing along with the others.

Cleaning up after the battle, they spotted movement on the hill and focused their firepower in that general area. In a short period of time the sappers were eliminated. But Bill was not sure if he could claim a kill. After everything settled down, they squabbled over who had killed the enemy. In spite of himself, Bill could not keep from arguing with the others about who should get recognition.

The whole confrontation ended as abruptly and unexpectedly as it had begun. The Vietcong accomplished their goal because once again the men in A Battery were in constant turmoil, wondering when the next conflict would start without warning. The persistent uncertainty created an atmosphere in which each man knew that he could die at any moment.

A Battery woke up to six fatalities and eleven wounded. Fortunately, most of the wounded were not seriously injured. Only two men were injured seriously enough to be airlifted to a hospital. Tim was one. He had received a piece of shrapnel in his right leg, requiring surgery.

"War is hell — but combat is a Mother Fucker."

~ ~ ~ ~ ~

When Tim woke up, his leg was bandaged. He couldn't move it so he was not sure how seriously he was wounded.

Even as he was being airlifted from the unit, he was laughing and joking with everyone. Bill and Dan stood around while the medics prepared to medevac. They gave him a hard time. He was wearing the same white underwear he had gone to bed in but it was bloody from his leg, which was burned from the blast.

"Tim, you'd do anything to get out of some work," Bill said.

"You guessed it, boy. I'm gonna go see some round-eyed women now! And be clean. Eat good. I'm gonna stay as long as I can. Try not to miss me." Tim laughed.

"Here," Dan said, handing Tim a book. "You can read this while you're in the hospital." The book was Ralph Ellison's *Invisible Man*.

"Thanks, Dan, I'll read it if I have time or get tired of watching those round-eyed women go to work on me. Who knows, maybe I'll end up an intellectual like you."

"Yeah, but don't try too hard," Dan said. "You'll get a headache."

~ ~ ~ ~ ~

Tim was airlifted to a hospital in Qui Nhon. Bill waited a few days and then decided to go and see him. He would visit the hospital while the others went on an ammo run and spent a couple of hours at a whorehouse.

Before Bill left, he went to see Long. He had not had a break since he'd started his job as a clerk over six weeks ago.

"First Sergeant Long, I would like permission to go on an ammo run so I can see Tim in the hospital," he asked.

"I wondered when you were gonna come around and make a trip like everyone else," the first sergeant smiled.

"I'm not sure I know what you mean."

"You're really going to make a trip to the house, aren't you?" Long, asked, glaring.

"No way," Bill denied. "I really just want to see Tim Edmonds and go shopping."

"We'll see. People will think you're not a man if you don't. Or even worse, if you know what I mean?"

"Thanks for the advice, First Sergeant." Bill saluted and left

Bill left for Qui Nhon with the others, still jolted by his conversation with the first sergeant. He realized that the others were surprised that he was coming with them.

"Perhaps I'm just being paranoid," he thought. "Why do they make me feel like less of a man because I don't want to go to the whorehouse with them?"

When they arrived in Qui Nhon, Bill left the others and went directly to the hospital. As he approached, almost a block away, he heard screaming and crying from the building.

He realized that it was coming from a room on the second floor and looked up at the source before going in.

"Will I have to pass by that room to see Tim?" He thought.

He asked a nurse in the lobby for Tim's room number.

"Second floor." She pointed to the stairs he would have to take.

As he climbed the stairs, the high shrill cries pierced all of his sensibilities. As he walked by the room, down the hall from the stairs, he saw shadows of men running through the partially opened green shutters covering the windows to the room.

When he passed the entrance to the large empty room, he saw eleven men running around the room naked. Immediately noticeable was that they had no hair anywhere on their bodies. It had been seared off their flesh. Their skin was scorched red and black and it was cracked and bleeding, literally hanging from their bodies, in pieces from their bones. There was blood everywhere, on the floor, smeared red and black on the white tile walls. Everywhere Bill looked was an expanse of blood.

"All these tormented warriors could do is run around the large empty room wailing and crying. Everything they touch caused them pain. Even the bottoms of their feet have been seared," Bill thought, unable to believe what he was seeing.

He saw an American nurse sitting at the desk located in the center of the entrance to the room. "How can anyone suffer so much pain?" he thought.

"They were hit by other U.S. troops with napalm. It's not unusual for this to happen in this guerrilla war we're fighting," replied the nurse coldly.

"But can't you do something for their pain?" Bill pleaded.

"We've given them all the morphine they can stand without killing them. All we can do now is watch and wait."

"You mean they're going to die?" Bill asked, unnerved.

The nurse nodded her head and looked down at the desk. It was impossible for her to say anything else to Bill.

"We will never be the same again," Bill thought. "What is manhood? Is it the first sergeant for visiting the house? The horror of seeing these eleven men is worse than any combat I've seen in a little over three months."

Bill was going crazy with anguish, not knowing what to do.

"Why the hell don't you give them some more pain killer? They're going to fucking die anyway! You know it and I know it! How can you sit there and let them be in so much pain? WHAT THE FUCK IS WRONG WITH YOU?" He stopped abruptly because he could see that she was crying. Her tears were falling on the paper in front of her.

Bill looked up again. One of the soldiers approached him and seemed to be reaching out to him. He was a slightly built young man and looked to be barely twenty years old. But it was impossible to tell what his race was because his body was so badly burned. Somehow he knew that Bill understood his anguish. He looked Bill straight in the eyes. Through his tears and pain, he cried helplessly. "Mama, Mama, Mama!" Abruptly he returned to the safety of the chaos with the other men because he had nowhere else to go.

Bill was speechless and standing alone. He looked up in anguish. He ran down the hall in the opposite direction and into a bathroom. He barged into the first stall and slammed the door behind him. He stuffed his shirt in his mouth and began to cry convulsively. Then he vomited into the toilet, flushed it, and sat down. He cried on the toilet for more than fifteen minutes.

After he stopped, he sat silently until his soul was finally at peace. He was not sure what had happened.

"Now I'm changed forever," he thought. "Going back to the unit after what has happened today. If I had known that I'd confront this, I would never have signed up for Vietnam. Now I know why some American soldiers become deserters."

But Bill still wanted to see his friend Tim Edmonds more than ever. He rushed to Tim's room. He could hear Tim's welcoming voice in the distance and picked up the pace of his steps and entered the sick room. There were three American nurses standing around his bed, changing the bandages on his leg. Tim sensed his friend's presence immediately.

"What are you doing here? You're not here to take me back so soon, are you? I kind of like this place," Tim laughed, chiding Bill for obviously admiring the young women.

"I came here because I was worried about you. I'm not sure why I did, now. You obviously don't need my help!" Bill laughed.

"Aren't you going to introduce us to your handsome friend?" one of the nurses smiled.

"You've been here not five minutes and you're trying to take over my territory," Tim replied to Bill.

"My name is Bill Freeze. How's my friend doing?"

"Oh, he's just fine. He should be back to the unit as good as new in a week or two. We'd better go now. I'm sure you two have a lot to talk about," another nurse said. The three nurses left giggling

"Tim, how are you, really?" Bill walked over to a chair next to the bed and sat down.

"You don't waste any time, do you? I've been worried about you guys being out there in the jungle without me— the Crusher! You know, in some strange way I miss you guys even more than my family. I mean, at least my family is back home in Tennessee safe. I can't get you guys out of my mind."

"Why don't you come back with me then?" Bill asked, smiling.

"It's not like that, Bill. I've had a lot of time to think here for the first time since coming to Vietnam. Being here's made me realize how awful we've got it in the field. It's good for me to meet the other guys here. Their stories are pretty much the same as ours. Man, it scares the hell out of me going back to the unit again! By the way, what's all that screaming about down the hall?"

"Oh, it's nothing really. Just some guys who don't know how to bear up to their pain," Bill answered uneasily.

Tim looked him in the eyes and said, "They won't let any of the patients near that room. Are you sure that's all it is? Listen to them yelling. It's been going on non-stop since late yesterday. I'll be glad when it's over."

"I'm sure it can't end soon enough for them either," Bill said.

"Enough of that serious jive," Tim said abruptly. "I got to call my wife and talk to her. She's just fine. I even got to speak to my two kids! I didn't realize how much I miss them. I'll see Annie when I go on R&R to Hawaii. You know, you can miss your woman every day for nine months and almost go crazy inside. But it only takes an hour to make up for all that lost time since we were apart, you know what I mean?" Tim smiled.

"You're crazy. Does your wife know that you're nuts?" Bill said, laughing.

"No sir, she thinks I'm the sanest man in the world, my friend," Tim laughed.

They continued talking for two hours in a light manner. To their surprise, reliving their war stories since coming to A Battery eased their tension.

Too soon, Bill had to leave to do some quick shopping before returning back to the truck to meet the others.

"Oh yeah, be sure and tell Dan that I've read almost half of the book he gave me. Tell him I've felt like the invisible man in this book many times. It has really helped me understand myself better. I don't get it all, so tell Dan I'll have some questions for him when I get back to the unit." He put out his hand to shake Bill's.

They gripped each other's hands tightly and didn't want to let go. "Thanks for the visit and take care of yourself. Tell everyone I said hello and I'm fine," Tim said to his best friend in the unit.

"Tim, you better get well in a hurry so you can come back with us. This visit has done more good for me than it did for you, I'm sure. Thanks again, Tim," Bill said.

"You'd better go now, little soul brother." Tim smiled and winked.

After Bill's visit with Tim he was feeling much better. Now he could ignore his conversation with the first sergeant from this morning.

"Besides, it will only make it worse if I allow myself to dwell on that asshole anyway," he thought, walking out of the hospital.

As he shopped, Bill reflected among the street vendors. "Vietnam is an exotic land with people from a unique culture. It's rapidly becoming a living hell for us. It's a place where our values are not respected. Is anything relevant here? What does it mean—this conflict? Maybe I'll become embittered after all like so many returning Vietnam vets. Perhaps Caldwell was right when he told Dan that he should just become like everyone else, a killer and fucker and a druggie. For the first time in my life, I can't say I know where to turn for the answer."

Extend Now!!

Hi Hi silver and away!

I've developed a new philosophy — dread only one day at a time

To be Fat is cool
I am cool
Real cool
Extra cool

— Budda

(where is ChubbyCheer?)

Happiness is humping
Racquel Welch—SLOWLY!

Bodda
mistake
extension
never
again ⟶ Do Dcau
Chubby Cheer

"alexander"
26 Jan 69

Some one Help me
Please......

PFC Johnson
Short
only
345 days to go

CHAPTER 7

What are they gonna do, send me to Vietnam?

TWO WEEKS LATER Tim returned from the hospital to A Battery and reported to the orderly room. No one was present. He decided to wait, knowing that Bill would return shortly.

His spirit was undaunted by the whole experience.

"I no longer feel invulnerable, but it could have been much worse. There's a good chance that it will happen again," he thought while sitting, waiting for Bill.

"However, this time I promise myself that I will not go off the deep end like before; no more drugs or the house. I can't get Annie and my children out of my mind. I talked to them one last time this morning before returning to the field. I'm so sorry I made the call. She fell apart when she found out I was wounded. It was worse when I told her my hospital stay is over. I'm back in the field now. For how long? Until I die?"

He remembered Annie's words over the phone that morning. Through her tears she had said, "I want you to know that I love you now more than ever. I don't care what you have to do to stay alive, just get home safely. Tim, whatever you have done or will have to do, just know that you are forgiven, and we will welcome you home with open arms. I love you and you are in our prayers every, every day. Call me again when you can. It does us so much good just to hear your voice. You are the love of my life."

Annie had hung up sobbing, not giving Tim a chance to respond to her. His soul was in the depth of despair.

He had thought after the phone went silent, "My heart's cries are unutterable. I didn't know anything could hurt so much."

He was not sure whether he would have the will power to keep away from the soul brother's decadence—the drugs, booze, rock-and-roll on the stereo every night, and trips to the house.

"What scares me the most?" He thought. "Not combat. Lord, I need strength and can't imagine where it will come from. I won't talk about it to anyone. They'll think I'm crazy. Or worse, they won't give a flying fuck about what I'm feeling. Besides, everyone else is carrying these same thoughts secretly. It would make more sense if they could share with each other. I won't. They won't."

As Bill entered the orderly room, Tim smiled and said, "How are you? Did you miss the Crusher while I was gone?"

Bill ran over and shook his hand and wouldn't let go. "Yeah, it's been quiet around without you here."

Tim laughed. "Yeah, that's right, when you go out to the bush, you can't leave without the Crusher."

"You haven't changed at all. Hey, you have a lot of mail here waiting for you but I imagine you don't care about that," Bill taunted, laughing too.

"Give that to me before I go crazy," pleaded Tim. "Man, I can't wait to read those lovely words from my favorite woman!"

Long and the medic entered the orderly room, returning from the whorehouse. Putting on his tough army bravado act, the first sergeant snarled, "Well, what the hell you been doing all morning, Bill Freeze?" He was drunk.

Bill said nothing and only looked at Long. Like the previous clerk, he was used to the lifer's meaningless tirades and would not give him the satisfaction of an answer.

Long went into one of his daily rages as he looked at the clipboard. "What the fuck is going on here?" He tapped the clipboard. "Eleven damn men are on an ammo trip? They don't need over four men for a trip like that. What in the hell would we do if we got attacked? We would be fucking defenseless. It is your job to make sure this doesn't happen again. I should write you up. You're supposed to monitor this kind of shit for me when I'm not around."

Still unaffected, Bill said, "Well, several of the men needed to pick up supplies from the PX."

"Yeah, hell yeah. The whole unit is going to come down with fucking VD!" yelled the first sergeant, now red-faced. "Now, don't you forget that when I'm away, you are supposed to be in charge. One of these days, Bill Freeze, I'm going to send you to jail!"

Bill changed the subject. "First Sergeant, I'm hungry. Permission to go the mess tent?"

Frustrated by Bill's lack of response, the first sergeant barked, "Ah, go eat. But hurry back, 'cause the medic and I have to make another trip this afternoon. We have to do some advanced reconnaissance."

It was not unusual for the first sergeant to visit the house more than once a day, especially if the captain was not around.

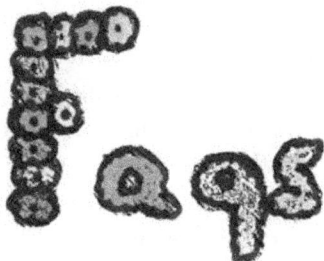

Bill grabbed his army combat gear and left with Tim for lunch. On the way he explained to Tim. "Of all the men in this outfit, Long is the worst offender for taking up his time at the house to visit his favorite girl. He may actually have a crush on this beautiful young French-Vietnamese girl, Gail. He was telling me that the mixed-race women are so beautiful they take his breath away. But both the French and the Vietnamese reject them. The first sergeant pities her. The only way girls like her can make a living is by becoming prostitutes."

"I bet the only hope for these exceptional beauties is for an American soldier to take them home, which won't likely happen. Though I bet the first sergeant promises her he will—the asshole!"

They laughed.

Back at the medical tent the first sergeant was talking with the medic. "I like that kid," he said. "Except that I think he might be queer. He never goes to the whorehouse! It ain't natural, I tell you!"

That was when Bobby came running into the orderly room with a pained look on his face. "Doc, I just knocked the fuck out of my finger with a hammer! Could you fix me up?"

"Sure," answered the medic. "I'll see you later, First Sergeant, I'll be back as soon as I can so we can go on our reconnaissance mission." He left to go to the medical supply closet. As the medic was working on Bobby's finger, Lowe entered the tent.

"Doc, all I need is some more Darvon," pleaded Lowe. "How about it? My head is killing me from working around the big guns today."

"Yeah, I know," snapped the medic, unconvinced, as he reached into his cabinet and handed Lowe a huge bottle of pills. "Take all you want." Lowe took a huge handful and put them in his pocket, then gave the bottle back to Doc. He left hastily without saying thanks.

"Yeah, I know what that fucking nigger wants," raged Bobby. "He's gonna drink, blow dope, pop pills, and shoot up all at once to get the maximum high. I hope the fucking nigger kills himself!"

"With any luck there'll be one less nigger for us to put up with," replied the medic as he continued to fix Bobby's injury. "You know, sometimes it's almost more than I can do to pretend I like them."

"Yeah, but they'd shoot us in the back, or visa versa, if we didn't need to depend on them to protect us. So we kill them with legal army issued drugs," Bobby replied.

The world is a whore and she keeps me.

After lunch Bill and Tim returned to the orderly room. Tim returned to get his gear and then reported to his section chief.

As Tim was leaving, the first sergeant stopped him. "Edmunds, I need you to go on a trip with me this afternoon. Would you drive me?"

Tim was surprised that Long asked him. "Sure, First Sergeant. When do you want to leave?"

"Right now, since Doc can't go with me after all," replied the first sergeant, smiling.

They left to visit Long's number one girl but in less than fifteen minutes they were back. Tim appeared at the orderly room tent entrance.

"What are you doing back so soon?" asked Bill as he looked up from his desk. "You just left!"

Tim whispered, "Let's go to the mess tent." As soon as they got ten feet away from the mess tent, Tim burst out laughing and ran inside to grab a cup of coffee.

Bill caught up with him. "What's wrong?"

Tim couldn't stop laughing but he finally calmed down enough to talk. "The first sergeant and I got ambushed by some Vietcong not half a mile down the road!" He started laughing uncontrollably again.

"What's so funny about that?" asked Bill blankly.

"Well, you see, we were heading down the road and we started getting a few pot shots aimed at us. The first sergeant told me to pull the jeep to the side of the road. So I jumped up to man the machine gun like I was stink on shit. And… and the mother fucker jams on me!" Tim started laughing again.

"Then I start firing the medic's M-16, and it jams too. Now all we have is Long's .45 pistol. What a fucking joke because we both know he won't be able to hit a damn thing with it. We were fucking defenseless! Well, next thing we're dodging the Cong's bullets and hugging the ground on the same side of the jeep. I start to get my ass under the jeep, and the next thing I know is that the first sergeant is pulling my black ass right back out again. Then he tries to crawl under the jeep with his .45, but he can't fit because his beer belly is too big." Tim was barely able to continue.

"It was the funniest thing I've ever seen in my life! I couldn't help myself so I started laughing. Then right in the middle of all this action he turns around and growls at me that he's going to send me to jail for insubordination. I had to stop laughing and start playing soldier again even though there wasn't a fucking thing we could do."

"What!" Bill laughed.

"We were fucking lucky because some Military Police came along right in time to save our asses. I know I should have been scared, but the whole thing seemed surreal for me, especially Long's beer belly. If you know what I mean?"

Tim and Bill both laughed uncontrollably. They returned to the orderly room tent and found the first sergeant sitting at Bill's desk. He was obviously steamed.

Chicken man – He's every where He's every where

"Bill Freeze!" growled Long. "I just received orders from Headquarters that they need a special status report for First Field Forces. You're going to be working late tonight. It has to be completed with no errors and delivered to Headquarters before midnight." He threw the order at Bill and left.

"Ain't that some shit?" said Tim.

"What can they do? Send me to Vietnam?" joked Bill. They started laughing again.

Finally Tim said, "I'll see you later, man. I ain't seen any of the guys in my section yet. Hell, I don't even think they know I'm back." He started walking. "Oh, by the way, if you start getting down, just think about me and the first sergeant's beer belly on our trip this afternoon." They burst out laughing again as Tim left.

Three hours later Bill was still busy working on the lengthy emergency special report. When he was close to finishing the first draft, he made one mistake and had to start all over. Now he was forced to work even later. He started the second draft, agonizing not to make another mistake. The only action in the orderly room tent was the sound of the antiquated manual typewriter pecking away.

Babies are better than bombs.

The girls back home are a scare comodity.

Accidents cause People.

CLiMAX

~ ~ ~ ~ ~

Late that afternoon in Gun Section #1 Bobby was reminiscing.

"Man, you know what I miss the most? Those Texas women who were more than willing to spread their legs for me."

"Yeah, I miss those round-eyed women too," agreed Sergeant Chen.

"You?" asked Bobby, looking at Chen in disbelief.

"Don't look so shocked. I'm married to a round-eyed woman back home," answered Chen proudly.

"All we have is some slant-eyed or mix-breed women, which we have to pay for the privilege of their company," griped another soldier.

"Yeah," agreed Bobby, "and they charge us twice what they do the fucking gook soldiers too!"

"Oh, that's because we have so much more to give, especially some of the black boys. I don't know how those little women take it all!" laughed another solider.

"You know Vietnam ain't all that bad," said Bobby. He leaned back relaxed with his arms behind his head. "I get all the free beer I want to drink, plus marijuana is cheap. And I get a good lay once in a while."

"You seem to get your rocks off even more when we get into combat," smirked one of the other soldiers who was sitting with them.

Bobby with an evil gleam in his eyes looked at the soldier and replied, "Yeah, except we ain't got in a good fight with the Cong for a while now. You know there's something about combat."

He spoke intensely. "I enjoy it more each time. I believe I'm lucky because we got hit fairly hard last time, and I was the only one around me that wasn't wounded. And I got fucking Charlie's ass good! I even took pictures of the pile of dead gooks before we buried them so I could send them to my father. He'll share them with my buddies back home. After our last combat I decided that I love to wake up to the smell of the Viet Cong's burnt flesh."

Everyone was shocked at the honesty of Bobby's remarks. There was a long pause in their conversation.

Finally Sergeant Chen broke the silence. "Let's drink to the girls back home!"

Everyone agreed. They lit up some smoke, guzzled some more beer, and descended into a drunken stupor which with their sincere dedication it did not take long to accomplish.

$ex

If you first don't succeed
Try, Try Again - - then offer
Her some - - - money!
(THE ROOT OF ALL EVIL)

~ ~ ~ ~ ~

Meanwhile Bill had been typing the lengthy special report without a break for dinner until around 2130 hours when he finished. The report had to be delivered to Headquarters Battery before midnight.

Bill contacted the FDC Command Bunker and asked them to tell Headquarters Unit that a jeep from A Battery would deliver the special report to the Sergeant Major. Caldwell answered the phone, and he was delighted. Bill was caught in a tough situation again.

"Oh, I'll be happy to tell them that two dumb mother fuckers will be delivering something to the Sergeant Major on a night that we've had two separate reports of incoming rounds from the enemy. Bill, I bet you're sorry right now that you decided to take the Company Clerk's position," Caldwell said on the phone.

"You are a fucking asshole," Bill said. "Just call HQ and let them know we're coming. I don't want our asses to get shot at by friendly fire."

Caldwell was ecstatic that he'd gotten Bill pissed. "Now let's be calm. I'll get everything taken care of. However, my suggestion is to bust ass as fast as you can."

"We will."

Bill found Dan first and Dan agreed to assist him. He had no choice but to ask someone to ride shotgun. Headquarters was located one mile down the road through several barbed wire barricades positioned approximately every 50 feet. The barricades were placed across the road at dusk to protect the units from the unseen enemy that used the road under cover of night.

They had no time to waste so Dan borrowed Lowe's M-16 rifle and rushed to Headquarters. They loaded their weapons. There had been earlier reports of incoming rounds. Unavoidably, they stopped seven times so Bill could move the barricades and Dan could drive. With each barricade the tension built. It was pitch-black and they were sitting ducks. The headlights from the jeep clearly gave away their position.

Also a gung ho American soldier could easily mistake them for the Vietcong, especially since there was only short notice announcing they were coming. Dan spoke the only words during the trip when he said "Only in Vietnam!"

Tomorrow What?!?!!

Despite everything the trip went smoothly. They returned safely. Dan jogged to the bunker and gave Lowe back his rifle. Relieved, they went to the mess tent to get a cup of coffee. There was always coffee available since there were men on duty 24 hours a day. As soon as they sipped it, a gunshot blasted within the perimeter of the unit. They took off running.

They heard someone yelling, "It's Lowe! He just shot himself!"

Dan and Bill ran to where they had left Lowe in the bunker. They found him clutching his left hand. He had wrapped his t-shirt around it. It was impossible to tell if it was a serious wound but there was no blood on the t-shirt.

"Maybe it's not too bad," Dan hoped.

The first sergeant entered. He'd been drinking. "What's going on here?"

"I was just cleaning my gun and I had my hand around the top of the barrel and the mother-fucker went off!"

"How did it get loaded?" demanded Long.

"Don't know," answered Lowe. "Maybe Dan Semple knows."

"I used his rifle when delivering the special report to Headquarters with Bill tonight," Dan explained.

"Were you two fired at?" snapped the first sergeant.

"No, but we were concerned because there had been two incidents of incoming rounds into the unit tonight," Dan answered reluctantly.

"I thought you two were supposed to be among the smartest in the unit. This just goes to show both of you that all that book knowledge is not going to help either one of you in this case! Both of you report to orderly room at 0800 hours tomorrow," the first sergeant said. Everyone was silent.

"This will most likely mean an Article 14 for both of you," the first sergeant screamed. "Get the medic to take care of his hand. I don't see any blood on the t-shirt so I don't think it's hurt too bad. He's still a dumb mother fucker for cleaning a loaded rifle!" He stomped out and went back to drinking.

"Do you think we're going to get an Article 14 for something like this?" Bill asked Dan.

Dan looked at Lowe, then at Bill. "Do you really think there's any doubt?"

Someone in the crowd started laughing at them. "Well next time, Private 1st Class Dan Semple, maybe you better be more careful who you borrow a rifle from." Everyone else began laughing at their undeserved plight.

Dan and Bill were powerless. They walked away from the crowd knowing that U.S. Army military justice would be served in a way that was unique to Vietnam.

"Dan, I think we should fight this. We were just taking necessary steps in case we had to defend ourselves. I'm sorry I asked you to come along with me," Bill said.

"Oh, don't worry about it. We'll have to see what tomorrow brings and strategize on how we're going to handle this situation. See you tomorrow. Try not to worry about it. Lowe is still a dumb mother fucker," said Dan. They went to their separate bunkers to catch some sleep.

Bill stayed up thinking. "Tonight for the first time I question my reasons for coming to Vietnam. Now, this is not what my best friend Chris McLaughlin would have wanted to me sign up for the draft for—to anticipate that I'd be caught in this situation—when I was stateside—fuck."

Meanwhile Dan wondered for an instant if he should contact his father. But he knew that it was not an option; somehow they needed to resolve this situation on their own. Dan decided that tomorrow he would need to become familiar with the U.S. Army's Article 14 policy.

"FUCK IT"

This year's election has been cancelled due to lack of interest.

(Vote For The Lesser Evil)

To Lowe, if I had a quarter for every word you wasted — looking good Budda

CALL A YELLOW CAB

CAB

Fuck The Army

Keep On Truck'n

Chapter 8: JUST SAYING NO

DAN AND BILL reported to the orderly room the next morning, but First Sergeant Long was a no show. Dan waited until 0900 hours and told Bill to go to up to the FDC command bunker. He would send for him as soon as the first sergeant showed.

When Long arrived at the tent around 1030 hours he looked rough. He ordered Bill to type up two Article 14's for loading their weapons without due provocation. As Bill typed the documents for himself and Dan, the hung-over Long grinned while rubbing his temples. He had a headache but liked watching Bill perform his duty both as clerk and as punishment.

But when the documents were ready, Dan and Bill refused to sign.

Pissed off, Long scolded them. "Now listen up. You are being instructed that if you do not sign, it could result in a court-martial, and you'll be tried for this incident." He paused. "You can call the army's bluff, but I guarantee you two will not like the results. Boy, if you like Vietnam, you're gonna love a court-martial. I'm telling you!"

Still they refused to sign. They remained silent and still during the first sergeant's lecture. Bill was used to staying calm during the first sergeant's furious berating.

"Sir, I am refusing to sign the Article 14," they each said just once during the exchange. At the end of Long's rant, when they knew they would soon be dismissed, Dan finally spoke up.

Though sheepish, he simply stated, "Sir, I am prepared to write to our congressmen, senators and the president. And if things really get bad, I will even go so far as to write Dear Abby."

After that they were dismissed. With his hangover Long could take no more.

"It's out of the question," Dan said to Bill as they were walking out. "Surely the U.S. Army will give in to reason this time?"

The dust and the heat hit them at once as they walked from the orderly room to the mess tent for a cup of coffee. They still had their duties that day.

"The whole situation here at this base is deteriorating. Now the question is how we are going to get a fair trial when the very organization that is accusing us is also the judge?" Bill asked Dan.

The gossip of the incident spread. It was no surprise to anyone in the unit that they were getting charged with an Article 14. However, it was surprising that Dan and Bill, of all people, were refusing to give up under the pressure. Without realizing it, they were gaining respect from the other men.

They requested to meet with Captain Biddle in the afternoon.

"I'm sure he'll be unbiased," Bill assured Dan. He had interacted with the captain many times as company clerk.

Biddle agreed to meet with them. They were instructed to meet him at the orderly room tent. Dan and Bill were both anxious about the meeting. Captain Biddle entered the tent carrying his M-16. They stood and saluted him. He returned their salute.

"At ease, men. Please sit down. How may I help you?" He listened to them intently.

Dan spoke first. "I'm sure you're aware that Bill and I have refused to sign our Article 14's. We're receiving pressure to sign them. However, we don't think it's fair."

Bill interjected, "Captain Biddle, we were trying to protect ourselves because there were indicators that we would likely receive enemy fire. I honestly think we were following the most appropriate measures to ensure our safety."

Bill proceeded to explain the details of the event: the special report he had to type, the late hour they had delivered it, the reports of incoming fire, the haste with which they had departed, borrowing Lowe's rifle, moving the barbed wire roadblocks, and the stoned Lowe's accident with the loaded rifle.

After listening to them for over a half hour, Captain Biddle smiled gently, paused, and said to them, "I understand that logically you are correct. However, the rules apply differently in the U.S. Army than in civilian life. Right now you are bound by the military's rules and regulations. One of the primary regulations while we are engaged in Vietnam states that you cannot put a round in the chamber of your weapon unless you receive permission from a higher authority."

Dan and Bill sank while Captain Biddle continued.

"It's unfortunate, but there is no front line here. It's not unusual for American troops to die from friendly fire. Therefore I cannot assist you in getting out of the Article 14, since this is one of the most fundamental rules that we operate by while in Vietnam. This is not a reflection of what I think of either of you, because I think that you are fine soldiers. However, there is nothing I can do to help, no matter how much I'd like to. You need to take the initiative to assure that the outcome is the best one possible. It wouldn't be good for something like this to appear on your permanent military records. My best advice is for you to seek legal advice from a JAG officer—a lawyer. Is there anything else?"

No one responded. They saluted and Captain Biddle left.

Dan said to Bill, "Well, I guess there's nothing else that we can do except to speak with a JAG officer. I think we need to begin our writing campaign. What do you think, Bill?"

"I never thought I'd be in a situation—this is bullshit... An Article 14—let alone a court-martial! I think the first sergeant enjoys watching me sweat this one out every day."

Extend Now!!!

~ ~ ~ ~ ~

For Bill and Dan the entire situation seemed more preposterous because Lowe had only powder burns between two of his fingers. It was impossible to blame him since he was deteriorating more rapidly each day. No one paid any attention to how far it would lead.

The day of the Article 14 hearing, without warning, Lowe completely lost it. While Bill and Dan were meeting with Captain Biddle, Lowe finally read a letter from his wife that he had received last week. It said she was leaving him for lack of financial support.

He was in his bunk, drunk, on speed, with a joint in his mouth, when he read the letter and screamed, "She's leaving me! I can't take it! The bitch! I can't take it!"

Through a drugged stupor Lowe grabbed a .45 revolver and began shooting at the other men in Commo Section. They rushed away to save their lives and hid behind some sandbags. Everyone was helpless and no one wanted to see Lowe hurt. Tim tried to reason with him from behind a pile of sandbags.

"Hey soul brother, give us that pistol, man! You don't want to shoot any of us!" Tim yelled.

"You don't give a fuck either," screamed Lowe. "Nobody cares! I've lost my woman, I've lost everything!" he sobbed. "And... and if I lose everything so are you mother fuckers!" He fired wildly again. Shots popped into sandbags all around the camp.

"Lowe, Lowe, stop it! You'll end up in jail, man!" Tim begged, lying on the ground.

Suddenly they heard more loud yells and cries from Lowe. The pistol fired another three times. Then there was a sudden quiet. Tim with helmet on poked his head over the sandbags. Everyone rushed to see what had happened to Lowe. They were sure he had shot himself.

They found him lying face down on the ground. Tim grabbed the pistol from his fist. They turned him over on his back to check for blood. There was none. His black skin was ashy white. His eyes were half open.

Everyone knew immediately what was wrong. Lowe had finally overdosed. He had a pulse but made no response. He had passed out and now started go into seizure. They radioed for the medevac unit to send a helicopter. Within a few minutes a helicopter landed and the two medics took Lowe away. Tim tucked the .45 in his waist.

Tommorow has been Cancelled.

Lowe returned to the unit within three days. No punishment was recommended so he returned to the field to continue his struggle without any help. He was a broken man. No one said anything about it to him.

~ ~ ~ ~ ~

Caldwell, Flower Power, Bill and Dan congregated in the back room of the FDC command bunker. It was always exciting to see how the Bitch Wall had evolved since they had last looked at it. It was a particularly joyful night for Caldwell and Flower Power since they were officially becoming short-timers at the stroke of midnight. In two weeks to the day they would be leaving Vietnam for the U.S.

The air was mixed with joy and sadness: joy on the part of Caldwell and Flower Power, sadness on the part of the men they would be leaving behind. This set the tone for an unusual conversation over their warm beers.

"Have any of you read *The Heart is a Lonely Hunter*?" asked Dan. "It's a sad and very poignant book."

"Yes, in college," answered Bill. "Another book like that is *Flowers for Algernon*."

"I read both of those on the beach in LA in the land of the big PX! All the characters are trying to come to grips with a reality that is far too big for them to handle," Flower Power added. "In *Flowers for Algernon* they all deal with hope, success, failure and ultimately bravery in facing the end."

"Yeah, yeah, yeah, but in *The Heart is a Lonely Hunter* there were insufficient returns for the protagonist's investment of himself, resulting in the personal bankruptcy and dissolution of the corporation… that is, corporation in the original sense," Dan disputed. "All those values you said ended up being ironic."

"You know," said Flower Power, "before I came to Vietnam I never thought I could survive a situation that I couldn't come to grips with. We're in danger of suffering from personal bankruptcy here. Yet I've done it without going too crazy."

Caldwell was relaxed that night, not his usual cocky self. He looked at Flower Power, smiled and proudly said, "Yes, we both have survived." He raised a peace sign with his right hand. He was finally letting down his guard.

Flower Power smiled back. He looked at Caldwell with affection. He had never allowed himself to before. He had been afraid he would lose his best friend to this war like so many others. "Yes, we have, Caldwell, except you seem so damn unaffected by this whole situation."

"That's right," Caldwell laughed. "And you still talk the same old intellectual bullshit with anyone who'll listen. We both made it our own way!"

"You know what I'm going to miss the most? The Bitch Wall," proclaimed Flower Power as he studied the wall.

"Yeah, maybe me too," said Caldwell. "It really says everything about our unit. Many times I've come up here at night by myself and stared at it and thought about what it all means."

"You're getting soft, Phil Caldwell," teased Flower Power. "I'll always remember it too. The Bitch Wall will always linger in my mind."

Everyone sat quietly staring at the wall for a few minutes. 'Like a Rolling Stone' by Bob Dylan was playing on stereo.

"It was a bitch about Lowe today," Flower Power said thoughtfully, breaking the spell. "I think everyone could see something like this coming for a long time."

"If you ask me," Dan said, "in a way he had it coming."

"Oh, bullshit!" Caldwell yelled, all fired up. "I'm surprised more of us don't go fucking crazy like him over here!"

"Dan, when the hell are you going to stop being so fucking judgmental?" Flower Power asked, disgusted by Dan's remark. "I really thought you were beginning to change."

"I'm not being judgmental," Dan insisted, on the defensive.

Bill spoke strongly to Dan. "You can't judge Lowe so easily. I know he does drugs, drinks, and runs to the whorehouse every chance he gets, but he's falling apart like the rest of us. Shit, it's all we can do to maintain any sense of normalcy. You think you can intellectualize your way out of everything, man. You can't! I know you can't. One of these days you'll see that all that knowledge you hide behind will lead you to a dead-end street!"

Dan was taken aback by Bill's outburst and struggled to appear unaffected. "I can't imagine any place that will lead me to a dead-end street," Dan replied coldly. "It hasn't so far, not even in this place."

"Oh, who the fuck cares?" Caldwell interrupted. "Look, it's getting close to midnight. Let's all celebrate! Two weeks, Flower Power! Two weeks and we'll be home! Two weeks and I'll be fucking my round-eyed sweetheart in New York City! Two weeks! Two weeks!"

Caldwell grabbed Flower Power and they gave each other a bear hug.

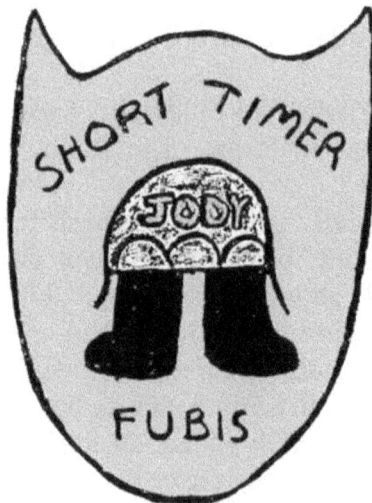

DON'T GET CAUGHT DEAD WITHOUT YOUR DOG TAGS....

Piss on it

Jones – Home Nov '68

I hate this Fuck'n place.

Wat now?

Chapter 9: NIGHT ATTACK

AFTER A 12-HOUR SHIFT together, Phil Caldwell left the FDC bunker with Bill. They talked about how excited he was to return home to his girlfriend and family.

"I even bought her an engagement ring while I was in Hong Kong with Flower Power," Caldwell said. Bill had never seen Phil so relaxed. He seemed like an entirely different person.

When they said goodnight, Phil said, "I gotta take a leak before hitting the sack."

He headed to the piss tube to urinate—a 50 gallon barrel cut in half, turned upside down, placed in the ground upside down, and filled with diesel oil to reduce the odor.

As he was urinating, he looked up and noticed a sky full of stars, more than he had ever seen in his life.

"So close that you could reach out and touch them," he thought. He was exceptionally high after smoking some really strong pot with Flower Power and the others.

"Tonight for the first time since I came to Vietnam, I feel everything is going to be fine. I feel all right," he thought.

He stared for a few more minutes after zipping up. Then he went to his bunk, located next to the entrance to the FDC sleeping bunker. He fell asleep immediately. He was fully dressed since he was too tired to take off his uniform after working the twelve-hour shift.

When the sappers came into the perimeter, they tried to disable the big guns and hit the bunkers where the soldiers slept. The FDC sleeping bunker was located immediately adjacent to the FDC command bunker where the men worked.

A sapper sneaked around the area, spied an almost imperceptible light coming through the entrance of the FDC sleeping bunker and threw a grenade in. It rolled under the bunk where Phil was sleeping.

He did not know what hit him. He took the full brunt from the explosion. The other men were not even scratched by the shrapnel.

Caldwell died with just two weeks left in Vietnam. Of all the people in the unit, he seemed the most invulnerable one.

The unit was caught completely off guard. No one thought or knew the enemy was preparing to attack them that night or any night. After the sapper hit the FDC sleeping bunker, the Vietcong hit with rockets and mortars. Then sappers attacked almost instantaneously to catch as many sleeping men off guard as possible. Everyone got up when the explosions started crashing through the camp.

Hernandez was on guard duty at the Commo Section's outpost. He was smoking a joint with the other men on guard duty with him. It was a very dark night, so dark you couldn't see your hand in front of your face.

Hernandez was taking a long and greedy puff when a rifle banged. Suddenly he collapsed. The men around him scrambled frantically to find a flashlight to see what had happened. Finally one of the soldiers fumbled around and got his Zippo lighter out. They shone it on his face and saw that he was shot in the middle of the forehead.

One of the men on guard duty with him got upset and yelled, "You dumb mother fucker, how many times have we told you not to take a hit off a joint in the open where the enemy could see you? They can see a light from a joint for a good quarter mile or more on a night like this!" He paused, collecting his breath from shouting. "You still owe me fifty bucks! You could have waited to die until after payday, you shit! Now I'll never get that money."

Everyone sympathized with the complaining soldier. They did not allow themselves to get sentimental about another man's death. It was just his tough luck. It was callous, but they had to keep their emotions in check to survive. They were in the middle of an attack, ducked under sandbags while sniper shots popped on the wall around them. They heard the mortars crashing in the camp.

Old soldiers never die—
young ones do.

Bobby was on guard duty at OP #1 when the attack took place. After he heard the first shots, he saw a sapper breaking through the perimeter and jumped him from above with his knife, stabbing him again and again, severing the man literally in half, laughing the whole time.

"Take that, you fucking gook," he said as he kicked the remnants of the body over and over again.

"Fuck you and what you stand for! I'll kill more of you than anyone else has before."

The other men on guard duty with him watched him in horror.

After that he looked like a crazed man stalking for more prey, breathing heavily. The flares were high in the air. Bobby and the soldiers scanned for movement within the perimeter. Spotting another sapper crawling by a bunker and preparing a homemade incendiary grenade, Bobby sprang up. He rushed the sapper, tackling and knifing him. There was a third sapper crouching behind a sandbag wall at the next bunker. Bobby rushed him too, thrusting a knife right in his throat as he tackled him and wrestled a grenade from him.

Then he ran 50 yards to the outpost and began firing the M-50 machine gun and combed the hill, killing everything in sight. No one could say for sure how many of the enemy he killed single-handedly. The M-50 left only shreds of evidence its victims on the ground. It was originally designed to be an anti-aircraft gun. It was so powerful that if it hit a person anywhere he imploded, leaving nothing behind except unidentifiable bits.

~ ~ ~ ~ ~

Bobby received a Bronze Star for his heroics. However, he was not exactly the kind of hero most of the men had learned to idolize in the past.

"Are all war heroes like him?" some wondered.

Bobby felt legitimized by the award.

"My Bronze Star is something no one else can fully appreciate," he thought after getting it pinned in a special ceremony a few weeks later. "It matters little what the others think. Besides, they're afraid of this place. Not me."

The men in the unit kept their distance from him as much as possible. They had seen what he could do in combat. They didn't know if he was nuts, like Lowe, and would turn on them.

He scared them more than the Vietcong did. They tolerated him during the attack. It forced them to face how war could destroy someone, and they wondered if they were not just like Bobby but were hiding it better. It was an unspoken truth that everyone delighted at the opportunity to kill the Vietcong during combat. It was impossible not to feel a deep sense of satisfaction.

"Because fuck it, if you don't kill them, they sure as hell will kill you at the first opportunity," Bobby explained to everyone.

Though We Be as Reprobates... → yeah - but tell me a better way here!

~ ~ ~ ~ ~

Flower Power had just admitted to himself how much he cared for Caldwell. He was afraid. He knew that he might die too, even with so little time left in country.

The morning after the attack he went through Phil's personal effects so he could send them home to his family. He found a picture of Phil and his beautiful girlfriend, and her engagement ring that he had selected in Hong Kong on R&R. Then he found a picture of Phil and him together when they had first arrived in A Battery. On the back was written:

6/16/'67
*My best buddy
George Morrison (alias)
"Flower Power!"*

Tears were running down his face.

Quietly he spoke to himself. "You S.O.B., why did you have to die on me? You were my closest friend here!" He became hysterical. He spoke out, alone in the FDC sleeping bunker. "Why did you have to come in my life? Now I'll have to learn to live without you. What about your family? I can't just send them this stuff; it's too impersonal. I know. I'll bring your things to your family myself on my way home. I won't let you down!"

He calmed down.

"You'll see. I thought that I'd finally grown numb to other people's death. I let down my guard for one second and look what happens. I'm so insane at this point in my tour of duty that I'm not sure how I'll ever readjust when I return home."

Then he thought, "The only way I can make it these last two weeks is to stay drunk and drugged up. Maybe time will go faster for me this way. Even if it doesn't, I won't give a flying fuck anyway! One week and four days."

Flower Power stood and popped a can of warm beer. There was a small collection of loose cans under Caldwell's bunk.

"This one's for you, Phil. I'll make your family proud. I'll let them know how much you meant to all of us here."

He sat back heavily. "That's a joke, isn't it? I'll have to lie to them. They don't have to know what insensitive bastards we've become over here!"

Flower Power's behavior became subdued. He was falling deeper and deeper into the abyss of alienation. No one questioned him to see if he needed help during his last weeks in the unit. They figured he was estranged because he was leaving to go home soon. But the inattention only pushed him further into the desert of hopelessness.

That night around the Bitch Wall, Flower Power said nothing. He thought in a deep drunkenness, "I've now completely permanently lost the reality of Vietnam. What is this place? One week: re-entering and readjusting to home… It will be painful if it can happen at all."

While the 'White Rabbit' by Jefferson Airplane played on the stereo in the FDC bunker, Flower Power with a joint in his hand would not let anyone know how Phil Caldwell's death had affected him. He did not tell anyone that he was delivering Phil's personal effects to his family before returning home.

"If I don't do this for Caldwell, I'll regret it the rest of my life. If I can do just one decent act to reconcile what Vietnam has become. It's my only hope for justifying what Caldwell has become," he thought while the other men goofed off with the Bitch Wall.

When Flower Power left the unit, he put on a display of confidence that convinced everyone he was fine, shaking hands with his buddies, wearing his uniform proudly before climbing in a helicopter.

Flower Power Doesn't Live Here Anymore

Chapter 10: R & R

BOBBY WAS THE FIRST of the four to go on R & R. He was going to Taipei, Taiwan, where there were always open slots. It was not as popular as some of the other destinations for U.S. troops to visit.

He chose to go on R & R early in his tour, hoping that he would get another chance to go again, as some of the other men in the unit had finagled.

Bobby left the unit, flew to Cam Ranh Bay, and hustled off to Taipei. He arrived, found a hotel, checked in and immediately started hunting to find a woman.

He felt set free walking down the streets.

"Like old times," he thought, strolling with a swagger. He was on the prowl, looking hungrily for the company of a young woman. He spied some beautiful Taiwanese girls hanging alluringly out of a door. As they watched him approach, they posed for him, hoping for some attention. He walked in the door and a mama-san came over to him.

"G.I., you want plaything?" she smiled inquiringly.

"Yeah, I want her to be soft, young and pretty," Bobby said.

"You look over there. See what you like," she said.

Bobby was exhilarated as he carefully scrutinized the women standing before him. He found what he wanted. Smiling, he said, "I want that sweet young thing over there in the red dress."

The girl smiled excited and gladly walked over to him. He put his arm around her and began pawing her.

"My name is Peggy. What is yours, G.I.?" she said enticingly.

"My name is Bobby." He gave her a kiss on the cheek.

"You like her, G.I.?" asked mama-san, tapping him on the shoulder. "She is one of my best girls. Very popular with Americans. She is $20.00 a day."

Bobby was completely taken with Peggy. "Do I get a reduced rate if I pay for a week in advance? I'll pay you $15.00 a day. Take it or leave it. I know that's the going rate."

"You run hard bargain, G.I. But you win." He gave mama-san the money and they left to see the sights of Taipei.

Peggy took Bobby around the picturesque city. They first went to the hub of Taipei where the Presidential Palace is located. This building was misnamed since Taiwan had no president, only a chief executive. Nearby New Park covered a block or two and contained the Provincial Museum where Bobby found interesting exhibits of Taiwan's history. He enjoyed the classical pagodas and gardens connected to the museum.

Peggy guided Bobby. He was fascinated by the crowded streets of Hwa Hsi, one of the main shopping areas. He was amazed that he did not find it oppressive like those in Vietnam.

They continued their tour with ease. She helped him order the delightful foods that are unique to Taiwan, which Bobby gladly tried. She pampered him in every way imaginable, especially during their nights together.

Everything was completely carefree for them. Without a doubt, Bobby knew that he had fallen in love with her and wasted no time in asking her to marry him. She was used to this question from the other Americans. She casually shrugged it off.

Still Peggy hoped that some G.I. would come and take her away from the world she felt permanently trapped in. It would have to happen before her beauty dried up, before she could no longer make a living at what she enjoyed doing. Peggy loved spoiling vulnerable men. This time she had almost convinced herself that she was in love with Bobby.

Later that evening over dinner Peggy explained. "I come from a small village and a family of seven children. Our father spends hours working their small farm raising rice. But it is barely enough to feed them. I receive only a small share of what I earn from mama-san. But I still have enough to send money back to my family. As the oldest daughter I knew that I would help my wonderful family. I know several other girls who have decided to do the same thing. I hope you understand."

Bobby grabbed her hand and squeezed it and smiled. They walked in silence back to their hotel.

During their second night together, Peggy was awakened by Bobby's yelling. He was having a nightmare, and she heard him screaming in his sleep.

"Turn around! They're behind you! Don't let them get you! Oh, they killed him! I'll get even with that mother..."

She began shaking Bobby to wake him, but had difficulty calling him from the dream. She finally revived him.

"Are you okay, Bobby?"

He shook his head yes. Then she kissed him and began drawing with her finger on his chest. He took her into his arms. Peggy placed her head on his chest and they lay awake for an hour, not saying anything before falling asleep again.

When they woke up the next morning, they were still embracing. Neither one mentioned the episode from the night before. Peggy took special care of Bobby. He welcomed her nurturing. He needed it desperately.

On the fourth night, while they were celebrating, Bobby was drinking more heavily. Once he had had enough at the bar, he ordered her to return immediately with him to their hotel room. Peggy was afraid. He was usually so boyish with her.

Bobby fetched a taxi. On the way back to the hotel, he violently kissed and pawed her. She was frightened. She wondered if she would end up mangled or dead like some of the other girls. At the same time she was even more afraid of leaving him, because of mama-san's wrath. Plus, in some deluded way she hoped Bobby had come to rescue her.

"Better to have a brutal existence with Bobby than to keep it going here," she thought.

The cab pulled up in front of the hotel. Bobby paid the driver. They hurried up the stairs to his room. He was drunk and pulling her by the hand. When they got to the room he locked the door behind them and stood in front of it. He leaned his back on the door with his head facing the floor in a drunk stupor.

"Take off your clothes!"

"Bobby, what's wrong? You are acting so strange!"

"I said take off your clothes! That's what I paid you for, isn't it?" He spoke darkly, almost whining, very drunk.

"Happiness is a ——> Warm Gun"

Peggy began to cry but submitted and stripped for him. Then she sat on the bed crying. Bobby was unmoved. He walked over to the bed and lay down.

On his back, he dragged her close to him. He mauled her to demonstrate his masculine prowess over the delicate Asian girl. He was not making love to her but was grotesquely relieving all his pent-up emotions on her. He expelled his fears, anxieties, stifled emotions, loneliness, hates, and crippling anger.

He was inflicting all this on one helpless woman. Through it all Peggy somehow understood Bobby's agony. She was paralyzed with fear. He squeezed her everywhere and savagely kissed her all over her body.

But after ten minutes of it she rebelled. She caught him off guard and pushed him away with her feet, sending him rolling on the floor. Bobby was livid.

"What will he do?" she thought, scared.

She became hysterical and began sobbing.

"Bobby, don't hurt me, please! I love you!"

Bobby was jolted by her last statement. He got a glimmer of what he had been doing to her. He ran over to the only chair in the room and began smashing it to pieces.

As he was destroying the room, he kept screaming, "I can't stand it! I've had enough! I can't stand it!"

The hotel clerk heard all the commotion coming from upstairs. He called for the Military Police. When they arrived they broke down the door and dragged Bobby away naked into the night, to cool off in jail.

As they took him away, Peggy cried out from the balcony, "Oh, Bobby! Oh, Bobby, I love you!"

Bobby would be sent back to Vietnam on the first morning flight. He also had to pay for the damages to the hotel room. He would not have to go to trial since the hotel manager did not press charges because of Peggy's influence.

The next day he was delivered to A Battery by the Military Police. It was not until he was back in his bunk that he realized how deeply Peggy had touched him.

"I'm in love with Peggy! I'm in love with a fucking gook!" he thought. He was shocked and pissed to be back. He had no way of contacting her again since he did not know the address or the name of the place where she worked. It was on her business card that he had left in the hotel room.

~ ~ ~ ~ ~

Without any previous notification, in mid-October the U.S. Army suddenly increased the allocation of men authorized to be sent to Australia every month. Many of the men in the unit had more seniority than Bill and Dan, but none had money available on such short notice. Most of the men spent all their monthly salary on drugs and booze, sophisticated electronic equipment, the house, or gifts for people back home that they purchased through the PX. Many had already gone on R & R to Australia.

The two allocations would go to waste if they weren't used. So Bill and Dan decided, Why not?

Eight days later they found themselves on a luxury airliner heading south towards Australia. They met other men on their flight who were excited about meeting white round-eyed women.

Bill and Dan noticed that there was only one black soldier on the plane.

"Sydney is primarily a white soldier's R & R," the black man explained to him. "Since it's more like home than the other places to choose from, most of us prefer to visit the Asian countries where brothers are more accepted."

They thought back sadly to A Battery. They had only just begun to understand the blacks' dilemma through their friend Tim Edmonds.

Dan slept and read most of the flight. Bill visited with the other men. He struck up a conversation with one of the men on the plane who seemed to know a lot more about what to expect in Sydney.

"Yeah, Australia is a great place. I've heard there are three women for every man. That gives us pretty good odds, don't you think?"

"It sure sounds like it. I heard they are really good looking too," Bill said.

"Yeah, and they must wear the shortest mini-skirts in the world. Why, I heard if you're behind them and catch them walking up a hill, you can see a glimpse of their panties!"

They laughed.

"That's nothing. Make sure you go to Manly or Bondi Beach. The women wear the skimpiest bikinis! The side straps have to be at least three inches wide or they get a fine!"

"It's for sure I won't miss the beaches. What about you, Dan?" Bill asked.

Dan shrugged, looked disinterested and continued reading.

"Yeah, but the girls know how to get around the law," continued another soldier. "They roll up the sides of their bikinis when the guard isn't around and unroll them again when he makes his rounds. Sounds like heaven."

"Yeah, it sure does," Bill said. "Most of all though, it will be good just to get away from Vietnam for a while."

Bill and Dan landed at the airport and went to check into their rooms at a hotel. Then they bought some civilian clothes at a store located off the lobby. They headed for long overdue hot showers and met two hours later. Both were amazed how much dirt oozed out of their skin. They showered until the water was clear coming out of their pores.

They spent their first two days seeing the spectacular sights in the city. They were amazed at the Opera House, although it was incomplete. Their days were full of visiting the beaches, museums and restaurants. But they went to bed early their first two nights since they were so exhausted from Vietnam.

On the third day, while at the beach, they decided to go out that night and meet some of the famous Australian women. They didn't really believe that they would meet any, but "There's no harm in trying," Bill finally convinced Dan.

They ended up at a disco bar where all the tables were interconnected by telephones. They felt as if they were back home, watching everyone dance in the carefree atmosphere.

Finally Bill mustered up the nerve to ask one of the beautiful Australian girls to dance. He called the woman on the telephone and she agreed.

She had a small frame and long flowing auburn hair, blue eyes, and the clearest complexion he had ever seen. Her name was Wendy. He thought she was the most beautiful woman he had ever met. He found her accent captivating. It was impossible for him to feel otherwise because she treated him with kindness and respect. But after a few dances, another soldier cut in on him so he backed away.

He didn't dance the rest of the evening but refused to leave when Dan decided to go back to the hotel. When Dan left, Bill just sat at the table sipping a beer, taking in the scene. When the bar closed, he saw that Wendy was sitting in a corner looking dejected. Bill held his breath and walked over. She looked up at him and seemed to smile with relief.

"You haven't forgotten me?" she asked, surprised.

"No, but you seemed to be having such a good time with the other soldier that I didn't want to interfere," Bill stuttered.

"You Americans! I'll never understand you people. If I had any sense I'd steer completely away from you men."

"Why?"

"You come here and we can't help but fall in love with all of you delicious looking men. Then you leave us broken-hearted, promising that you'll return for us after your tour of duty is over. Of course, none of you do. I suppose we really shouldn't expect you to return. It's not fair to either of us." She was flirting with him now.

"Yeah, I suppose you're right, but I'd still like to get to know you better. Is that okay?" Bill asked, half shy but half sure of himself.

"Oh yeah, that would be divine, as long as we don't have any expectations of each other," Wendy said.

"That's great to me! I know it's late, but let's begin with a cup of coffee some place."

"I know of a café near the beach that's open 24 hours."

She took his hand and they wandered slowly to the beach, chatting along the way. Bill found out that she was a commercial artist who worked for an advertising firm. They continued until dawn. Wendy decided she had to go home to get some sleep.

"But I'll return with a car at 10:00 A.M. and bring a friend along for Dan," she promised Bill. She gave him a kiss on the cheek and smiled. "Remember, no expectations! Let's just have fun and enjoy each other's company for your next four days here."

Bill left her excited. He could not even remember how he made it back to the hotel. When he got back, he asked the clerk at the front desk to buzz his room at 9:00 A.M. Before he went to his room he left a note on Dan's door so he would be ready.

Bill was up before the desk clerk called. While he was getting dressed, Dan knocked on his door. Bill called for him to enter, figuring he was upset with the sudden plans. But Dan found it exciting.

Bill and Dan were waiting in front of the hotel at 9:45 A.M. Wendy and her friend arrived at 10:00.

"This is Cecile," said Wendy.

She jumped in the back seat and Dan fell in close behind. Bill got up front with Wendy and they darted away for a short jaunt west of Sydney, to Katoomba, the main resort area of the Blue Mountains. From there they rode the Scenic Skyway Gondola, which traveled on a cable high above the Jamison Valley floor. They spent the whole day enjoying the beauty of the mountains.

Bill and Dan were captivated by the beauty of Australia but even more by the warmth of the women.

"These ladies have graciously volunteered to be our tour guides," Bill explained to Dan, who was shy but smiling.

"Yeah, but mine is the better one," Dan teased Bill.

Wendy and Cecile showed them Sydney. After a while Dan started arguing with Cecile playfully about philosophers.

"So you're both intelligent and a Christian. You almost convince me that you might be right—an existentialist and Christian in the Kierkegaardian vein!" Dan laughed with Cecile in the back of the car.

Walking down boulevards, sometimes Wendy and Bill discussed deeply the immorality of war, love, family, hopes, dreams, and fears.

"I've never met a woman before who breathes as much passion for life as you," he confessed to her.

There was never a lull in their light-hearted conversation, except when they felt that the mood called for a restful silence.

On their last night together they went to the infamous Les Girls, a restaurant in the Kings Cross neighborhood where the performers were boys.

"It's a variety show with young and not so young female impersonators, very talented and stunningly attired," Wendy had explained to Bill on the drive there. "Campy humor awash with double entendre. All the singing is excellent."

"Why'd you choose this place?" Dan asked Wendy.

"Oh, be zany, G.I.," she told him.

The meal and show ended too quickly. Bill ate a French fry and thought of the reality of tomorrow and Vietnam.

"Hey Cecile, I want to show Bill my favorite beach. Can we meet you two at breakfast?" Wendy asked with a wink. She grabbed Bill under the table and whispered to him, "Don't you want to get those two alone?"

Bill was in love.

After they paid their check, they went their separate ways. Cecile and Dan walked around King's Cross enjoying the crowd. Wendy and Bill drove off in the cool Sydney night.

"This is just like Greenwich Village! Have you ever been to New York, Cecile?" Dan asked excitedly.

"I've been once. But Dan, I've so enjoyed our four days together. I want to thank you very much," Cecile told him.

"Yeah, it's been wonderful, hasn't it? I can't believe that I'll be back in Vietnam tomorrow."

Cecile stopped walking. She looked into Dan's eyes and kissed him. Dan was surprised.

"Cecile, thank you. You have no idea how much I needed that." He pulled her close and let the crowd walk by as they embraced.

"Dan, let's find one of those pleasant little restaurants and sip a cup of coffee." She smiled.

"That sounds perfect. I couldn't be happier."

They continued walking in silence. At a small diner they ordered their coffee. Neither said a word until the waitress returned with their order.

"I've grown to respect you over the last couple of days," Cecile said tenderly. "Though I still don't understand. How you can return to Vietnam without faith in God?"

"Oh, that. I resigned myself to the fact that Vietnam is but a short stopping point in my life." Dan paused. "It's frightening at times. But my life back home was secure. I have absolute control over who I am and where I'm going. I don't need God. I'm satisfied living my life in the way I was raised. When my life is over, that's the end of it all, I suppose. But I have no regrets really. Over all, up until Vietnam it's been quite pleasant."

"I can understand completely how God can become negated out," she said. "But I don't believe in Him because of my family or anything like that. For me, everywhere I turn intellectually, I seem to be led back. You see, I find the theories limiting. At best, when they're carried to their logical conclusions, they each leave you in the abyss. Surely you must realize the limitations of man intellectually?"

"Yeah, of course I do. But it doesn't frighten me. I welcome it since it makes life more fragile and therefore more beautiful. It brings intensity in my life… for me. My life is more beautiful because it's dependent entirely on what I choose to do with it. Therefore I'm in control of my life, and I believe I demonstrate considerable control under the right circumstances."

Cecile took Dan's hand.

"Dan, as a friend, I ask you to realize that no one's life can be kept in complete control, even under the most seemingly secure circumstances. Let's call it a truce!"

"Okay, let's spend the rest of the night enjoying your city and visit some more of your naughty all-night cabarets," Dan laughed.

"I know the place. It's even kinkier than Les Girls!" They left their coffee almost untouched as they started strolling around the neighborhood.

"You know, Cecile, my Vietnam experience may have taught me how to love." He put his arm around her shoulder and they continued walking.

He began a speech. "In an extraordinary demonstration of two different worldviews, gallantly challenging each other, resulting in reaffirming their original beliefs…"

He stopped and kissed her in the street.

Sunrise at Bondi Beach was more breathtaking than anything Dan had ever seen. Perhaps it was just the presence of Cecile. He was not sure. They walked barefoot on the beach, arm in arm, hoping the moment would last forever.

On the plane Dan thought, "Can I now face returning to Vietnam more easily after Cecile? I'm freer for some reason and not exactly sure why. I'm indebted to her because otherwise, in my private world, my Vietnam, where will she be? Who can I tell things to in Vietnam?"

"Denial of our creaturely openness and sharing in being results in a radical infidelity to the human condition." (Marcel)

Wendy and Bill found themselves walking along the beach where they had spent most of their first night together.

"It's been wonderful, hasn't it?" asked Wendy.

"Yes, it's been more wonderful than anything I ever could have imagined. I even think I've broken our bargain and fallen in love with you," Bill responded.

"Bill, please don't destroy the moment. It's been glorious to spend these few days with you. I hope that you'll always remember it for what it is. Unfortunately, it can be nothing more even though I wish it could."

"I know, you're probably right, but how can you be so callous after all we've shared?" asked Bill, pained. "I love you!"

"I'm not being callous. You're being unfair! Let's savor our last few hours together," Wendy insisted.

"I'm sorry. Of course you're right. Will you spend the night with me, Wendy?"

"I'm with you now," she smiled and blushed. "Whatever do you mean, soldier?"

"Would you spend the night with me in my hotel room?" asked Bill, blushing and turning away.

"And ruin my lily white reputation?" she retorted, pretending to be indignant.

Bill drew her near, embraced her and kissed her on the lips.

"I've got no other way of saying it. Words are inadequate at this point."

He stopped, pulled her away and looked her in the eyes. "Please, I need you tonight. I want to make love to you all night. I need you, Wendy, like I've never needed anyone else before in my life!"

Laughing, she threw her arms around him and kissed him. "I thought you'd never ask!"

They walked away clinging to each other and drove back to the hotel. Wendy and Bill reached deeply within themselves to share everything possible through their bodies. When they rested between sexual interludes they continued through their discussions, which they delighted in almost as much.

At 7:00 A.M.. they got a phone call from Dan asking them to meet Cecile and him for a champagne breakfast.

"We absolutely can't refuse since you're treating everyone," Bill said on the phone, naked between sheets with Wendy.

"Okay, pack your things and put on your uniform so we can save time and have a leisurely meal. We've got to catch a 12:30 P.M. flight." They arranged to meet in the lobby at 8:30 A.M.

Wendy and Bill raced to the shower to see who could make it first. It was a tie. After their long shower together, they got dressed.

Bill dressed in the bathroom. When he stepped out of the bathroom in his uniform, Wendy looked shocked. She slowly walked over to the window and started crying. Bill rushed over.

"Wendy, didn't you say that we had to keep this light-hearted?"

She put her head on his shoulder and continued to cry. "Oh, my dear sweet soldier, to think that someone as sensitive and loving as you has to go back to that awful place is almost more than I can bear. Please forgive me for ruining the happy mood."

Tears fell down his face too. "Thank you. Thank you very much. Maybe that will keep me from becoming hardened like so many others."

"Yes, I know. I've met some of them. Oh, don't change, Bill. Please don't change!" They embraced. Wendy couldn't stop crying because she realized "what lies ahead for my friend," as she later told Cecile.

Wendy

The phone rang again. It was Dan.

"Hurry up if you're coming!"

They rushed downstairs to meet Cecile and Dan in the lobby, their spirits running high again. They ate slowly, sipping champagne, and finished just in time to get to the airport. Wendy and Cecile drove them and watched them board the airplane with the other soldiers. They did not leave until the plane took off and was out of sight.

Before leaving, they reconciled themselves to the fact that they would most likely never see each other again. They didn't make a promise to write. The two Aussies only requested that the men would tell them when they had arrived home safely. Bill and Dan promised.

~ ~ ~ ~ ~

Tim was beside himself with anticipation about meeting Annie. Like a lot of married men, he chose Hawaii to spend his R & R with his wife. Annie had arrived the day before.

She chose the Royal Hawaiian Hotel, which had been built in the 1920's in an understated Spanish Mediterranean style.

It was more expensive than most of the other hotels, but she wanted nothing but the very best.

On her first night she couldn't sleep. She was so excited about seeing Tim the next morning. She rose early, bathed, and slipped into a new outfit which she had purchased to please him.

She looked at herself in the mirror and said, "Please God, let this be a perfect time together. Let's not have any of our nonsense get in the way this time."

Before leaving, she checked the room one last time to make sure everything was ready for Tim's arrival. It needed one final touch. She went over and opened the window facing the ocean so that a cool breeze would be blowing in the room when he entered.

It seemed to take the taxi forever to get to the airport. She arrived an hour before his flight was due. She paced back and forth in the main terminal, agonizing over each step, too antsy to sit down. But the plane was on time and she did not have to withstand the tension of waiting.

When the plane landed, Annie saw Tim descending the stairs. She was shocked. Her big 6' 2" hero must have lost 30 pounds. She swore she would not let him know she noticed. She ran to him and caressed him. They kissed each other and filled each other with hope for the next few days together. They were so hungry for one another that they could barely control their emotions until they were alone.

"You look great, Tim! Let's blow this joint and go to our hotel room," Annie exclaimed, smiling.

Tim picked her up and swirled her around. "Woman, you are just what the doctor ordered. Take me away. I am completely under your control."

They ran and caught a taxi. When they arrived at the room, Tim tore off her clothes. He kissed her from the tip of her head to the toes and back again. Then he picked her up and set her down on the bed.

"Woman, I am going to bring the max on you like I never have before!" Tim said as he pulled off his clothes and stood before her naked.

"The scar on your leg doesn't look as I expected, Tim. You are still the most beautiful man I've ever seen," she said.

For a while, nothing else in the world mattered to them. Their fire consumed their loneliness for each other. They could not stop until time for supper. Annie made reservations for them at the hotel's famous Monarch Room.

They ate dinner and watched the Hawaiian extravaganza. Then they took a long walk alone on the beach in the moonlight. They talked about their children, Johnnie and Georgia. Annie decided in advance not to ask Tim anything about Vietnam but let him bring it up on his own. It was as if they had never been apart and had grown together through their extended separation from each other.

The following days they visited the tourist attractions, Pearl Harbor, Iolani Palace, the Polynesian Culture Center, the Punchbowl, and the aquarium. They spent their mornings at Waikiki Beach.

The beach was crowded but the bathers and sun worshipers were amusing to watch as they passed in view. They walked from the public beaches near Diamond Head of Moana, all the way past Fort De Russy Military Beach, and to the Hilton Hawaiian Village.

"It's just good to be part of this decadent crowd," Tim said after a long silence during a walk.

A few of the beautiful women flirted with Annie's husband. Tim welcomed their attention and smiled back. It was a bitter reminder of their early stormy years of marriage. She tried to make a joke of it and not let it dampen her spirit. She felt she had to forget that he would never change his flirting with other women.

At night they enjoyed more of the shows at the local hotels and the Polynesian style revues. After the shows they danced away the evenings. Then they rushed back to their room to stockpile for the future, as Tim put it.

On Sunday Annie wanted to go to church with Tim. St. Andrew's was a church dating from the time of the historic Hawaiian monarchy's affinity for British style, even though it was a Gothic structure that was more akin to the churches of France. They were not Episcopal but Annie felt that it was important. When they left the service Tim told her he felt very at peace with it all.

On their last night together, they went to the luau at the Royal Hawaiian Hotel. It was no less corny than the other luaus.

"But the setting is so lovely we can't help but enjoy ourselves," Annie convinced Tim.

But at the party they were tense. The atmosphere was wild. Annie excused herself and went to the restroom. While she was away, another black soldier's beautiful wife asked Tim to dance.

While attempting the native Hawaiian hula dance with her, he saw Annie reappear. She turned around abruptly and ran away. Tim excused himself and chased after her. When he found her on a couch in the lobby crying, he put his arms around her.

"Annie, Annie, I'm sorry. I'm so sorry. I just forgot myself."

"You really didn't do anything. It's just that I don't want to share you with anyone else tonight. It just made me realize that I'm losing you again to Vietnam."

"Remember the Hawaiian word for love?" Tim asked smoothly. She shook her head yes. "Well, I aloha you very very much."

"Aloha"

"Oh, kiss me, you fool!" she said, smiling.

"What do you say we make ourselves scarce at the luau? Let's go upstairs now. You know what I mean," he whispered to her.

"Yes, I know exactly what you mean. But I tell you right now, I'm not letting you sleep tonight!" she said.

They rode the elevator to their floor and hurried to their room. Annie went into the bathroom and slipped into a skimpy negligee she had been saving for their last night together. It was Tim's favorite color, yellow. When she stepped out, he was already naked and waiting for her in bed.

"Lord, woman, you are more beautiful to me than any woman in the world," he said proudly. "Jesus knew what he was doing when he brought you into my life." She walked over to him slowly and sat on the side of the bed.

"I am going to make you as happy as you can possibly be. I don't know how, but I will give you more than I have given you ever before," she whispered.

He began kissing her back as he removed her translucent gown. She started thinking that she might never sleep with Tim again after tonight. She hoped that everything she was feeling could be concentrated into the one act.

"You are the only man I have ever loved," she said.

Tim memorized every part of her beautiful body. He barely whispered, "Annie, your eyes open my soul to love, your brown hair pleases me with its soft texture, you teeth are perfectly matched, and your mouth is scarlet and your words soothe my very being. Your cheeks, woman, are full, smooth and flawless. Your neck! Ah, yes, your long lovely neck is slim and strong. Your breasts are soft and lovely! They excite me so that I could get lost in them forever. I especially love your firm nipples, which crown them in all their glory. Annie, the curves of your body are round, womanly and intoxicating. Your belly is well rounded with no lack of joy for me. Your body is the work of the Master's hand, girl. I'm truly held captive by your beauty because I find no blemish on my dark skinned woman…"

Dawn swooped into the midst of their euphoria. Before rising, Tim held Annie in his arms and cherished their night together. She could tell he had something to say to her but she couldn't imagine what it was. He began but his words came with great difficulty, since he had never been comfortable expressing his feelings.

Annie sat up and looked him in the eyes. "My dear sweet man, this week with you has brought me more happiness than most people deserve in a lifetime!" She kissed him on the cheek. She was gently crying. Her tears fell on Tim's face. She wiped them away tenderly.

"Annie, I know this sounds stupid, but my time with you here in bed has been just like going to church for me. Those Episcopalians got nothing on us when we make love. Let's do it again! I don't need breakfast. You are all the nourishment I need right now!"

"Anything for the man I love!"

They mixed open cries and laughter. Unifying everything they were feeling.

Neither could ask to halt so they ended up running late. They grabbed a quick lunch on the way to the airport and had to run to the loading zone for Tim's plane. All the while Tim kept whispering "aloha" in Annie's ear.

As Tim left, their emotions were not as raw as at the airport in Knoxville months ago. They knew now that no one else could take each other's place in their lives. This was all they needed to know. Annie and Tim realized they could ask no more from each other.

Tim walked to his plane, turned back and waved goodbye to Annie.

Annie waited until the plane flew into the distance. Then she returned to the hotel to pack and get ready for her flight. As she was about to leave the room, her emotions swelled up inside her. She sat on the bed and wailed, "Oh, dear God, please bring my Tim home safe to me! I need him. I couldn't go on living without him!"

She did not know how long she cried. She stopped only when she felt completely purged. Then she was ready to leave their room. She caught a taxi to the airport.

"Nothing will separate us again," she thought, finding her seat on the plane, "if we can just make it through the next three and half months."

Us Texas boys are
gonna take over.

My prime of Youth is
but a frost of care.

"All the lonely people where do they come from; all the lonely people where do they belong?..." (Beatles)

The Song of Songs

Let her kiss me with the kisses of her mouth for her love delights me more than the rarest of wines...

Chapter 11: DARKNESS BEGINS

THE WORD CAME in that Bill and Dan's Article 14's were cancelled. The reason given was that Bill, acting as the man in charge, had given the direct order to load their weapons. However, most people believed they won because they had refused to back off being charged unjustly. There was a rumor that Captain Biddle had spoken up for them and gotten them off the hook because of their excellent records.

Captain Biddle handled it as he did everything else, in a discreet and gentlemanly manner. In the army everyone was a pawn and was required to follow orders or there would be consequences. It was not unusual for American soldiers never to know the reason they had to follow orders, but they were required to execute them blindly.

The news that the Article 14's were called off did not improve Dan's morale. Although it seemed impossible, he was becoming more alienated from the other men in the unit. Even Bill could not get through to him. After the death of Caldwell and Flower Power's departure for home, he had changed drastically. Everyone knew why but ignored it. To Dan, it was becoming apparent that Vietnam was a place whose reality was too large for him to control through intellectual theories.

Since returning from Australia, he had never readjusted. Now his primary release was writing to his girlfriend back home and receiving letters from her.

Cathy,

Thank you for your letters. I am not sure how I could make it without them. You help me to keep in touch with reality, as I knew it before I came to Vietnam. I find that there is no one that I can talk to anymore since Flower Power left. No one else here stimulates me intellectually. I think most of them find it a lot of nonsense.

I blame the U.S. Army less and less for our situation. I don't even blame the United States government anymore. History has a death grip on our country, teaching us that we are no different from any other nation which has ever existed. How could we fool ourselves for so long into thinking that destiny and righteousness would always be on our side?

The Army is caught in a war they are not allowed to fight to win, so we play asinine war games over here. In the face of this, the Army gets put up front and has to fight hard to keep up the pretense. As a result, the whole war becomes more and more hypocritical each day. The U.S. Government is caught in a desperate search for an argument to justify the American involvement in Vietnam. Therefore the U.S. Government deceives the Army and the Army is forced to betray the soldier. And even the most simple of us sees the tyranny of this hollow mockery that has caught all of us without warning.

How will this special race of men that has served here be affected? Even more frightening is how will we affect society once we have returned home? If our human spirits remain undaunted, perhaps we shall be an asset to our society. If not, I can't imagine, and do not want to imagine, what might happen to us. Probably we will continue to be rejected and remain suspect by the rest of society. Even I will be one of those that will be permanently judged for what I have done.

I must go now.

Always,
Dan

P.S. Thanks for the books that you sent me last week. They are my only source of companionship since returning from R & R. I have always wanted to read Atlas Shrugged *by Ayn Rand. I will start it this evening.*

~ ~ ~ ~ ~

After returning from Sydney, Bill felt unsettled. He was bored and did not know where to turn and decided to go to the house like everyone else.

"Maybe this will help me," he thought on whim. He had been invited on an ammo run.

With weak resignation he signed up. He said nothing about his decision.

He left with the others early in the morning. He wanted to be back by lunch and not interfere with First Sergeant Long's schedule. He rode to Qui Nohn with the others in the back of the truck bed. He said little.

"No one thinks anything about my coming along this time," he thought, watching the countryside pass by. "They figure that I'll be visiting the hospital or the beaches."

On the way to Qui Nohn, Bill thought about how he was going against everything he had been taught. Yet at this point nothing made sense to him.

Fuck it, he thought. I'll find out for myself once and for all.

When they arrived in Qui Nohn, he left the others and hunted for a house. It did not take long since the streets were lined with them. He entered the first one he found and did not take the time to notice the name. The first girl who caught his eye led him away, holding his shirt.

"She didn't ask any questions. Has she seen many others as desperate as me?" he wondered.

She led him into a tiny cubicle at the end of the hall. It was not much larger than the cot-sized bed in the room. Its cardboard walls had been painted with enameled bright pink and powder blue. The rooms were not soundproof. He heard the grunts and moans from other partners up and down the hallway.

She started unbuttoning his shirt and kissed his chest, all the while smiling. "You are very pretty, G.I. The prettiest G.I. I've ever seen."

She walked over to the cot and took off her clothes. He was stunned. Naked, she looked like a slightly overweight pre-adolescent girl with no breasts.

She's barely entered puberty, he thought. She had only three long pubic hairs. He wondered if she was even a teenager.

"How can I have sex with a child? Fucking hell," he whispered. So he did not go through with it after all. He gave her some money, more than she initially requested.

"Get out of here," he ordered and pointed out the door to the cardboard cubicle. Startled and a little afraid, she dressed hurriedly and ran out the door.

Bill sat on the cot. From the window, he could see the "pay-for-a-fee" lover running frantically across a field behind the house.

"What the fuck has this war done to us?" he thought. "She was forced into degradation for economic reasons, while my reasons are because I'm so lonely and need the stupid affection from anyone that cares about me. I'm sure both of us would have done things differently under other circumstances. I want to be with someone I love. With Wendy."

Bill buried his head in the cot and cried. He tried to muffle his sobs but soon realized that no one was listening.

"Even if they hear me, they don't care."

He cried more now. There was no need to muffle his sobs. His tears did not comfort him anyhow, only made him more aware of his isolation. On the way back to the unit he wondered if he would ever have the courage to allow himself to feel anything again.

For every woman that makes a fool out of a man. There's a woman who makes a man out of a fool.

~ ~ ~ ~ ~

The ammo run stopped at the Base Exchange at Phu Cat Air Force Base. They could literally buy the same American goods that were stocked at any large discount store back home.

Bill jumped out of the truck. It was only his second time going to the Base Exchange since arriving in Vietnam. The place was air-conditioned and there were items for sale that he had all but forgotten about. As he was turning a corner into another aisle to buy some snacks, he saw three sparkling clean airmen.

He looked them in the eye. They stopped immediately, turned around, and walked in the opposite direction. Bill was startled but understood their reaction.

He had been in the field for nearly nine months now and his mere presence frightened them. His appearance had changed dramatically since arriving. He was no longer a clean-cut young man. It had never happened to him before. A glimmer of how people will respond when I return home, he thought. He left the Base Exchange without buying anything.

When he went back to the truck, he waited for the others and said nothing to anyone on the return trip to A Battery. He was relieved when he got back. It was familiar now. On the ride back, he simply stared mindlessly out the back of the truck.

~ ~ ~ ~ ~

On the same morning, Tim, Bobby, and Sergeant Chen were on sandbag detail. They had hired some "friendly" Vietnamese to fill the sandbags for them. They were paid for each bag they filled. Bobby had to keep an accurate count so that they were not overcharged. Today the unit's mascot was with them. She was a nine-year-old Vietnamese girl named Linda. She was extraordinarily bright and one of the few Vietnamese who spoke almost perfect American English. She served as an interpreter when they needed to hire Vietnamese for a work detail.

"Ah, I hate this God-forsaken hole," Bobby grumbled. "This mother-fucking place! I don't know why we are here to save a bunch of gooks. I'm so sick and tired of seeing only gooks!"

"Hey, man, cool it," Tim said. He had Linda up on his shoulders while he was smoking a cigarette. "Linda is my number one girl, and besides she can understand everything you say."

"I don't give a damn. I'd run her down with my three-ton truck just like any other gook if she got in my way on the road!" Bobby yelled as he walked away, proud and taking a puff from his cigarette. "I can't wait to meet her in the house in five years. I can't wait."

Linda walked over to Bobby and looked him straight in the eyes and said, "G.I...G.I....you number one hundred million fucking dud!"

"Why that little gook bitch!" Bobby screamed, trying to grab Linda. "I'll fucking get even with you!"

Tim grabbed her and put her behind him, protecting her from Bobby. At the same time, Chen held Bobby back.

"Look, man, you deserved it," Tim shouted.

"But I ain't gonna let a little fucking gook girl get the best of me!" Bobby snarled, trying to get away from Sergeant Chen's hold.

"Cool it, man! Besides, we gotta hurry back because in about an hour the Donut Dollies are going to be coming to A Battery," Tim said, looking at his watch, hoping to cool Bobby down. "You know, those round-eyed Red Cross girls that bring us coffee and donuts out to the field. If we don't hurry, we'll miss it, man."

"Let's hit it, Bobby. Let's go!" Chen said.

"Sergeant Chen, and you a married man?" Tim teased.

"Over here, think again, man! What I want from them has nothing to do with marriage!" Chen exclaimed.

Vietnam is a bummer.

~ ~ ~ ~ ~

Tim was sitting alone at a table in the mess tent. Bill came over and sat with him.

"You know, if you hadn't come and sat with me, I would have busted out crying," Tim confided. "I don't know what's wrong but my stomach is all tight inside today."

"Yeah, I know what's bugging you. I heard about it. You were afraid to let Bobby drive the truck back to camp so you drove."

"Yeah, that motherfucker," Tim said, beating his fist on the table, almost in tears.

Bill was surprised. He reacted protectively because everyone was staring.

"Let's go outside. There are too many honkies in here," Bill said.

Tim looked around. Both black and white GIs were eating lunch in the mess tent. He and Bill left and went to an outpost.

No one said anything for five minutes while Tim was crying uncontrollably but quietly, unable to talk. Then he put his arm around Bill.

"Thanks for not letting me make a damn fool out of myself. I'm okay. But I was driving down the road and that son-of-a-bitch Bobby… he went kill crazy! First he took a chain and tried to hit an old female gook. Thank God he missed her. Then he took a board and knocked one of those gook men dressed in black off his bicycle. He went flying into a rice paddy! Well, that didn't bother me too much since he looked like he might be a Vietcong. Then, you know, Mama-san down on the LZ. He got her little boy with the...."

Bill nodded.

"Well, Bobby took a sandbag and threw it at him while we were moving at around sixty miles per hour. That sandbag hit little Tommy right in the chest and spun him in the air five or six times. He fell and got right up and took off running crying to Mama-san! You know every bone in his little body was probably broken. I couldn't help but think about my children when I saw him hit that little boy. What are they going to do to Bobby?"

Bill shrugged and smiled ironically. "Nothing. They'll probably give him a promotion." He jumped up, trying to lift his friend's spirit. "Hey, let's go and see the Donut Dollies. The An Kai girls are here today!"

Tim sprang to his feet, wiping his eyes. "Well, all right!"

~ ~ ~ ~ ~

HOORAY FOR THE AN KAI
GIRLS!
Love In - Reasonable Rates
(＄)

They ran over to a small platform in the middle of the unit where the Donut Dollies were located. The air was charged with energy.

"I told you things are better when they come, even if you don't actually get to talk to them," Bill said.

Every man in the unit appreciated visiting with them. The An Kai girls were Red Cross and friendliest with the ordinary enlisted men. They did not run after the officers like the other Red Cross girls. They also did not charge as much money if they decided to turn a trick. Many of them returned home much richer than when they had arrived in Vietnam.

Sally was the ringleader, and on her second tour of duty in Vietnam. She was around twenty-seven years old and not especially good looking, but she had a personality that warmed the soldiers' hearts.

"Well, here we are, men!" she announced from the small makeshift platform. "A whole USO floor show—except all of us have round eyes!"

All the men laughed.

"Hey, each time we come here, either this platform gets higher or you men are getting lower!"

Bill and Tim laughed and whistled from the crowd.

"Pretty soon you'll know that I don't wear any panties in this hot weather!"

She got them going every time.

"We planned a special show this time. No show on the stage, but we'll definitely give you a show that you want to see—offstage!"

She strutted around on the little platform, smiling and teasing the men.

Tim heard the phone ringing in the orderly room. He ran over to Bill, who was busy talking to the other girls.

"Hey, your phone is ringing."

Bill immediately ran over to the phone and answered.

"A Battery, Specialist Freeze speaking, how may I help you?" He listened. "You want Captain Biddle? Yes, sir, wait one."

He ran to the captain's bunker. Soon they were both running to the orderly room.

"You say it's the Battalion Commander?" Captain Biddle asked.

"Yes, sir," Bill answered.

"Captain Biddle speaking."

Bill could tell the message was serious. Captain Biddle put down the phone slowly.

"We're moving out first thing tomorrow morning."

"Where?" Bill asked, astonished.

"North. Tell Sally and her crew to get going immediately."

"Right away, sir?" Bill asked. His heart sank.

"You heard me. Right now!" Captain Biddle ordered.

Bill ran over to the girls while Captain Biddle made another phone call. He pulled Sally aside and whispered the news to avoid a commotion among the men.

"What?" Sally yelled. She jumped back up on the platform and called the other girls to her. She whispered her plan to them and they agreed with her strategy.

She was about to give this one all she had.

"Attention, attention, please! It is Christmas Day in A Battery! We had another unit that we were going to visit, but we are going to cancel our visit for you boys!"

Everyone was ecstatic. Captain Biddle entered, unnoticed at first.

"News has come that we'll be moving out again tomorrow morning. But not without some very special goodbyes from us!" She looked over at Captain Biddle, waved and smiled. "Oh hello, Captain Biddle."

All the men jumped to attention. Captain Biddle smiled.

"Yes, that's right, men. We'll be moving north close to the DMZ. We've just received orders from Battalion. Carry on, girls. But remember, Sally, you must be out of here in two hours!"

He walked off. The men shouted for joy because the Donut Dollies' presence would help them forget about tomorrow.

There will be target practice today at 1000 hours * 10 pt. – for old women & children.
5 pts. – for men.
1 pt. – for any cong.

*(The only prerequisite is that you must be scared out of your mind!)

on the rag

COUNT ME IN!

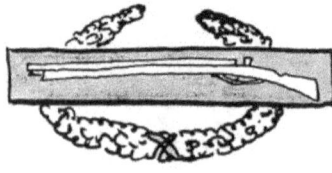

Roman Catholic morality is not opposed to heart transplant as long as their is absolute certainty of conscience.

Chapter 12: MOVING NORTH

THE PLANS CHANGED HOURLY. No one knew what their final destination was, including Captain Biddle and First Sergeant Long. They were constantly on the radio waiting for orders. The instructions came piecemeal.

At one point each of the battery's two leaders received contradictory orders. Captain Biddle had to call back to Battalion to determine which was correct.

"Everyone is wondering if the army has any idea where it's going. Do you think we're in an army war game? First Sergeant, do you have any idea where they might be sending us?" Captain Biddle asked. He and Long were riding in the same jeep.

"I don't have the slightest fucking idea," the first sergeant replied. "But I think our asses are in trouble. It's my hunch we're being sent north because the Vietcong is making a move."

"Well, that's not comforting to say the least. I suspect they're not exactly sure where they're sending us either. If you're correct, they're probably trying to figure out where strategically we can do the most damage. What do you think?"

"That makes a lot of sense to me, sir. It would be typical army bullshit," Long laughed.

"Were you ever in a situation like this in Korea, First Sergeant?"

"Hell yeah, but at least there we had a definite front line. For the most part we knew where the enemy was. Here any fucking minute a sniper could be hiding any place. It drives me fucking crazy that I don't know where those little bastards are," Long said in frustration.

"I probably wouldn't have phrased it like that, but I know exactly what you mean," Captain Biddle smiled.

"Let's just hope that they don't stick us out in the middle of nowhere. Shit, that would be it for most of us. The

Vietcong up here are tough; they're nothing to laugh at. I heard that the Russians and Chinese are training them. You think that's true?" the first sergeant asked.

"I think there's some truth to it, but who knows for sure? They've been fighting a war so long—hell, they're much better prepared than we are in guerilla warfare."

"Yeah, why in the hell don't they come out and fight us like real men? Then we could beat them fair and square."

"Well, right now we have to worry about where they're sending us. Hopefully we're going to know soon. The farther we go north, the more difficult it will be on our men. I want to make sure that we get as many of them home alive as possible. It's moments like these that I'm especially burdened by my job."

First Sergeant Long agreed. They didn't speak for a long time. They only talked when they received instructions from Battalion.

"No matter where we end up, at least I... we'll be relieved when we know our final destination," Long said after they received an order an hour later.

The unit in jeeps and trucks passed through An Kai and Pleiku and continued heading north, moving closer to the DMZ. The villages that they passed were war torn. Each was bleaker than the one before. Homes had been patched back together numerous times. The new patches reminded them of the devastation.

"In the name of freedom," the first sergeant said to Captain Biddle, who responded with only a stern look.

At one point the air was actually swollen with the smell of gunpowder. The day was humid. The sky was gray and overcast.

Two dozen Catholic schoolgirls walked down the side of the road together in formation of two lines. Two French nuns walked with them. One was leading them. The other was the last in the loose formation. They were the appointed guardians protecting the young girls. The schoolgirls were dressed completely in white. Their split skirts flew gently in the breeze.

"How can anything which speaks so simply and yet so strongly of a stability that does not seem relevant here survive in all its purity?" Captain Biddle thought. He was experiencing a vision of serenity more beautiful than anything he had ever witnessed. It was breathtaking, stirring thoughts of home and the things he had left behind. "Virgin beauty in the combat zone," he thought. At the same time Long tipped his helmet to the nuns. He held his M16 by the barrel, upright, with the rifle's butt resting on the floor of the jeep.

From the two-ton trucks everyone watched them in complete silence.

Why Are You Here?

But when they were out of the village, Captain Biddle and First Sergeant Long confronted the realization that they were still heading north. They kept driving another couple of hours. Then without warning they got an order on the radio.

They were told to pull off the main road onto a narrow road that was no more than a path into the jungle. Both sides of the road were lined with mangled, burnt out U.S. military vehicles.

"The men who had been in these abandoned vehicles... who will be next?" Captain Biddle thought.

The jungle encased them on all sides. They continued down the road. In sections it was almost as dark as night in the thick foliage.

"If we're attacked now, we're fucked—defenseless. I can't see shit," the first sergeant said. Biddle said nothing for five minutes.

"We've got to stay on this road for another hour before we finally come to a clearing in the jungle. That's our destination," Biddle said.

It was an isolated landing zone called Renegade. They were completely surrounded by an impenetrable jungle.

"Great! These men not only face an enemy they can't see, but this invisible force is also fucking trained," yelled the first sergeant.

The Vietcong in this area were called Chuck, since they were the equivalent to the U.S. Army's Green Berets.

Ain't this SOME SHIT?

Yeah man heavy

Short

fired of this"

MoM

①–Flower Brother's Association–①

C.B.

E₂ Coward slept here.

Would Jesus drive a chevrolet? Is the electric tooth brush a parody on humanity?

Beethoven suchs in B minor

1ˢᵀ nation rules

If you drop that crow one more time, you're out of the parade.

apples are apples, plums are plums

Pot

R.D.

Mary Jane

Chapter 13: LANDING ZONE RENEGADE

FOR THREE WEEKS the unit had been at Renegade. They had arrived in early April, a month before the monsoon season. But this year the rainy season came a month early. The men were literally up to their knees in mud. They were supposed to be at Renegade for only one week, but when the rains came, the big guns' tracks were trapped in the mud. The armored vehicles had sunk two or three feet and were completely immobile. It was impossible to get any traction to leave Renegade.

They were stranded at Renegade until the tropical downpours stopped. In spite of all the rain there was a shortage of drinking water. What little there was, the kitchen used to heat the C rations. Their drinking water came mostly from the muddy puddles they walked through. Worse, the unit had received no mail for over a week. This was bad for morale.

The infantry and artillery units were stealing food from each other since there was little to be found. The C rations were airdropped. Some of it landed on the perimeter of the landing zone but some fell in the bush for the Vietcong.

A Battery was successful in getting the other units out of the bush safely. With so much against them, they were still proud of the job that they had accomplished, protecting the other American soldiers. In the three weeks at Renegade they had provided the artillery cover necessary to hold the enemy while the other units fell back.

In that time everyone knew how important it was for them to be accurate when firing the artillery shells. They shot dead hits on Chuck without hitting American soldiers. It was easy to make a small miscalculation with one of the big guns and kill Americans with friendly fire. But this did not happen.

Now that it was A Battery's turn to move south to the safety of base camp, heavy rains came, and the earth swallowed up their heavy equipment in mud.

Keep smiling;
    IT MAKES PEOPLE WONDER.

~ ~ ~ ~ ~

A Battery had been informed that a general from Battalion and his party would visit the unit. They were anticipating congratulations for their excellent performance defending the other units. They were isolated deep in the jungle and far from American reinforcements. A Battery was the only major target left for Chuck to attack, and there was an ominous feeling among the men because it was inevitable.

Two hours before the big brass was anticipated to arrive, the U.S. Air Force began bombing the outside of the perimeter with napalm. Everything beyond the camp was engulfed in 30-foot clouds of fire. Thick plumes of black smoke rose in a circle around them. The Air Force did this to assure the big brass would be well protected while visiting the unit. It would be impossible for the Vietcong to attack while being pounded with fire.

"You know, Bill, it just doesn't make sense that the big brass is coming here," First Sergeant Long said skeptically.

"Something up, First Sergeant?" Bill asked.

"Maybe they're going to give us our last rites!" He laughed. Then he left with Captain Biddle to meet the general, whose party was scheduled to arrive by helicopter at 0900 hours.

We have done so
    Much with so Little
    We can do anything
        WITH NOTHING.

Captain Biddle and First Sergeant Long watched as the battalion team pulled an unexpected stateside spit-and-polish inspection. The big brass checked out each section methodically, then inspected each man with meticulous scrutiny. Everyone was shocked by the display of authority. Even the lifers could not believe what was taking place.

"This makes no sense," Captain Biddle said quietly to First Sergeant Long. "How can the big brass visit our unit under the protection of the U.S. Air Force and not even bring some fresh food or water? What are they trying to prove to us?"

Everyone except the men working on the big guns or on guard duty stood in formation to greet the general's party. In front of everyone, the first thing the general said to Captain Biddle was "Why aren't the men in A Battery in their authorized U.S. Army full uniform? I thought you were supposed to be the show unit of this battalion. Right now I wouldn't want anyone to see you."

Humiliated, Captain Biddle simply answered, "Yes, sir."

Everyone was shocked, wondering what happened to getting recognized for a job well done. The relentless barrage of napalm stopped immediately when the party flew out of sight a couple of hours later. Everyone in A Battery was pissed. Captain Biddle and the other lifers assembled in the orderly room tent. Bill was busy typing a report in response to the inspection.

"We're in enemy territory!" First Sergeant Long bitched. He was enraged, pacing back and forth.

"Yeah, I know, the big brass was here!" Bill replied sarcastically.

"Freeze, you're beginning to think just like me!"

"I didn't expect that, sir," Bill said, sitting down on a cot.

"Neither did I," Captain Biddle said, shaking his head.

"It's gonna look like shit for the both of us, ya know? I'm sure this is gonna get placed in our permanent records," First Sergeant Long said angrily.

"Yes, I know," Captain Biddle replied.

"You know what that son-of-a-bitch of a Sergeant Major did to me?" Long asked.

Captain Biddle shook his head no.

"Well, here we are in one of the most God-forsaken spots in Vietnam, and he comes up, and he puts his spit shined boots next to mine, and he asks me why mine don't look like his! He pulled that shit in front of the whole fucking formation!"

This is your dam — keep it clean.

"RAT EXIT →

How Long will it last? ——
that is a good question.

man is great, but everywhere you see him in chains.

"If that Sergeant Major ever puts his boot next to mine, I'll stomp on it!" Captain Biddle said, out of character. "They didn't bother bringing us food or water for the troops but somehow they found room in one of the helicopters to bring us three new recruits. Man, I'm concerned for those unlucky kids. I wish they had the opportunity to be at our base camp for at least a couple weeks. Hell, it was bad enough there."

A soldier from the Commo section entered the tent and handed the First Sergeant a radio teletype message.

Long read it. "We just got a message that the chaplain won't be able to make it in," he announced. "You know, we could always depend on a Catholic priest to come in and give us service. Shit, I'm not a Catholic, but I sure in hell would have had my ass at Mass today. Hell, everyone goes there to make peace when they're afraid they might die. You know, sir, when the chaplain goes AWOL, it's time to start fucking worrying!"

They all laughed out of terror.

One of the lifers sitting next to First Sergeant Long nudged him. "You know, First Sergeant, if things get any worse, I'm going to put in for a transfer to Timbuktu!"

They all seemed slightly relieved and laughed a little more loosely.

"Listen, I just remembered that the Sergeant Major wants us to take down all the pictures of naked women before he makes his next visit," another lifer spoke up. "Don't forget that was a direct order!"

"What the hell does he think we're running here, a Boy Scout camp?" First Sergeant Long fumed. "Besides, that pansy ass told me he's not gonna visit us again until we were in a different position. He doesn't like getting his boots dirty, I suppose."

"Oh, by the way, the only section that came out okay in the inspection was the Commo section."

A sergeant from Commo section beamed. "Yeah, I was sitting up cool, laughing at the big brass tear you honkies up!"

Then Long went to get the duffle bag with mail which had arrived with the big brass.

"Bill, we have a few pieces of mail that need to be delivered to the different sections. Most of it is scorched because it was in a helicopter that was shot down trying to deliver it. Although it's a couple weeks late I'm sure the men will enjoy reading letters from home. Some of the letters are burnt so bad that they'll only be able to read half their letter. But a little news from home is better than none at all."

~ ~ ~ ~ ~

Tim,

Everyone is fine here. The children pray for you every night before they go to bed. Georgia is doing especially well in school this year. Her favorite subjects are math and science. I can't believe it since neither one of us enjoyed those subjects.

My mother took some pictures of us at Sunday dinner a few weeks ago. I hope you like them. I think you can tell how much they have grown since you saw them last...

Your loving wife,
Annie

Bobby:

I hope that this letter finds you well. Your father told me to tell you that he enjoyed the pictures that you sent for him to show your friends. I didn't see them; he told me that they weren't for my eyes to see. That's okay; I didn't want to look at any pictures of war anyways...

I just want you to come home safe. Just remember that you are in my prayers every day. I wish you would write, we haven't received a letter from you for over three months. Your father said I should not worry...

Love,
Your mother

Dan:

Please remember to keep involved in the activities that were so important to you when you were back home. I was concerned that you were losing interest in reading and keeping your mind active...

I am especially happy that you enjoyed reading Atlas Shrugged. *I know it was a life-changing book for me. I know I identified with the main character. Because I think the many rely totally on the productive of our society. I think it was Wendell Wilkie who said, "Only the productive shall be strong. Only the strong shall be free."*

I think the book represents this philosophy very well...

Just get home safely.

As always,
Cathy

Bill:

I know you didn't expect to hear from me so soon, but I think about you often. I do hope that you are not in a dangerous place. Everything I hear on the news makes Vietnam sound like an awful place...

Cecile and I went to that little restaurant on the beach that we enjoyed. We could not stop talking about both of you. We think about you often. Please tell Dan that we said hello...

Your loving friend,
Wendy

After Bill had finished delivering the letters, he decided to visit a large group of men sitting together. For the first time, all the races and sections were sitting together engrossed in conversation.

Bill noticed that when men were close to death they were close to each other. Now there was no reason for them to maintain any artificial barriers. Differences of religion, race, or educational background were totally irrelevant. No one had any idea how long they would be stranded in the jungle. If A Battery was forced to stay throughout the monsoon season, they knew it would be impossible for all of them to survive.

"Bill, what are you doing here?" Sergeant Chen asked. "You're supposed to be in the orderly room."

"What can I say? They can write me up. By the way, how did it go here?"

"Well," Tim started, changing his voice to mock the General's, "the first thing the General asked me was, 'Soldier, where is your helmet? Why haven't you gotten a haircut?'"

"Yeah, he asked me why we hadn't policed the area," Chen added. "He said there was too much litter and debris in our area!"

They all laughed, saying, "litter and debris" over and over again.

Tim in the general's voice again said, "'Soldier, why don't you have your mosquito net up? Don't you know that you might get malaria?' Shit, don't he know that I want malaria so I can get to some place dry and clean? It would be great to recuperate in one of those hospitals again with all those American women."

"Yeah, one of them took off my helmet and ripped off my camouflage cover!" another soldier added.

"Why? Let me hear it," Chen asked in disbelief.

"Yeah, 'cause I had 'Love and Peace' and 'Make Love, Not War' written on it. I also had a heart on it with my girlfriend's initials on it. I guess he figures love is a dangerous thing."

"Well, I'd like to see one of them sleep here one night in the fucking rain. You sleep all night on an air mattress and when you wake up you roll off into three or four inches of water! And then you have to wear wet clothes all day!" Bill lamented.

"Wet!" Chen yelled. "Wet wouldn't be so bad. It's being up to your ass in mud all day!"

"I don't know why in the hell they didn't ask us about the jungle rot that all of us have on our feet from being in the mud twenty-four hours a day. I really don't think they give a shit about any of us," Bobby said. They all agreed.

Tim noticed that one of the new recruits was sitting quietly with them. He looked very young, slender, around 5' 6", and very clean-cut next to them since he had just arrived from the U.S.

He smiled at the new recruit and said, "Aren't you one of the green troops that arrived in the helicopters with the big brass? I think we should call you Blondie because of that color of your fresh buzzed hair."

The young soldier nodded shyly.

"I think we should indoctrinate him like the other troops when they go out to the field. Everyone, let's get some warm beer to toast Blondie."

They agreed, got beers, gathered around the new recruit and began singing to the tune of 'Camp Town Races' with good-natured fun. The recruit was obviously enjoying the warm welcome.

You're going home in a body bag,
Doo Dah! Doo Dah!
You're going home in a body bag,
Oh Doo Dah Day!
Shot between the eyes,
Blown off both your legs,
You're going home in a body bag,
Oh Doo Dah Day!

After they completed their song, they poured a portion of their beer on the new recruit. Everyone laughed. They shook his hand and welcomed him to A Battery. Then they gave him a beer to drink and everyone drank a toast to him.

"May you keep your head low when I'm blasting the enemy," Tim toasted.

Blondie told them he was eighteen years old and from a small farm near Lancaster, Pennsylvania. He was the youngest of six children and the only son. He entered the service right after graduating from high school early because he needed to use the G.I. Bill to pay for college. He had to because his family could never afford to send him. He said his family was very proud that he was serving in Vietnam. He had been assigned to Gun Section # 1. Sergeant Chen was delighted and picked up the new recruit's duffle bag and took him to meet the other men in his section.

~ ~ ~ ~ ~

"How about a beer?" First Sergeant Long suggested. "This is the only good thing about their visit, we can get drunk and forget about our misery! It's a good thing that misery loves company because we're the most miserable fucking men in the world today, boys!"

"Hey, First Sergeant," one of the lifers yelled, "when we get to San Francisco on our way home, we're going to the first bar we see and say'n two beers!"

"Well, after today I'm gonna hang a sign on my ass, and you know what it's gonna say, sir?" First Sergeant Long asked Captain Biddle.

"What is that, First Sergeant?" Captain Biddle responded, smiling.

"Open season on the First Sergeant's ass! I'm going home!" They all laughed. It was the first time that Captain Biddle had let loose with the enlisted men. He figured at this time there was no point keeping a professional distance. Everyone enjoyed his company and his sense of humor.

~ ~ ~ ~ ~

Tim got up and jogged over to his bunk and took out something hidden. He returned looking satisfied with himself. "I've been saving my marijuana stash for a special occasion. Let's not let this little shit hassle us!"

He sat on the cot and focused on rolling it up.

"Here we are in Vietnam fighting against an armed hostile farce!" Bobby stated, waiting for Tim to pass his stash.

"Hey, that's good," said Dan, astonished that he was actually agreeing with something Bobby had said. "But who's the bigger farce, the U.S. Army or Chuck? One's as big a farce as the other."

"Say, Bill," Sergeant Chen asked, "how can you stand being around the First Sergeant all the time?"

"Do you remember the clerk before me?" Sergeant Chen nodded. "Well, I asked him the same thing, and he told me, 'Freeze, this is just one of the many things you're going to have to learn to live with in Vietnam.' But you know what?" Tim added. "He ain't all bad. He's prejudiced but he tries to be fair. Anyway, let's keep rolling that stuff as fast as we can smoke it. Who knows about tomorrow? I bet we get hit hard tonight! I say fuck it all!"

"Tell Someone Who Cares"

SAY YOUR THING!

The Lord giveth and,
The Lord taketh away,
The Lord is an Indiangiver.

Things could be
worse we could be
hung-up on drugs.

Drive carefully,
they are after your
Heart.

4th section rules!

Is this place
for real ?

God is dead,
    Nietzsche.

Nietzsche is dead,
    God.

Peace

"So much depends
upon a small red
wagon among the
chickens in the
rain."
    (William Carlos Williams)

Love

Chapter 14: BEFORE THE ATTACK

ANOTHER MESSAGE was received from Battalion. It was anticipated by everyone after the visit from the big brass that morning. The message indicated that Chuck had completely surrounded A Battery and was planning to attack Landing Zone Renegade.

Since they were isolated from other American units, it was almost guaranteed that they would be attacked in large numbers with a well-executed strategy. Everyone assumed that the big brass had known this when they had inspected the unit so methodically.

It was obvious to the men that the army was powerless to stop the inevitable onslaught. The big brass continued the tyranny of its masquerade through the ludicrous stateside spit and polish inspection on the battlefield.

It was impossible to evacuate everyone from the landing zone before the attack. If an evacuation was initiated, Chuck would likely commence the offensive immediately. That would mean the death of even more American soldiers. The U.S. Army was forced to leave all the men to defend the insignificant landing zone, hoping their numbers would increase their odds of survival against Chuck.

The men were afraid to verbalize what they were feeling. It was impossible to admit to each other that they were powerless. They reflected silently. Who cares about us? Where can any of us turn? Where can I turn?

They pondered this as they made preparations around the LZ.

~ ~ ~ ~ ~

Dan: "Why do they call me Pencil Neck? What do they want from me? I am the fastest and most accurate statistician in FDC, figuring the correct firing direction for the big guns. What else can I give them? I wish I were home! My kind of man does not belong here. War is for animals and that's what all these men are—animals! They've reverted to a primitive level of behavior. But I won't. I couldn't face myself if I did. They even try to make me feel guilty because I'm an intellectual.

"But something is wrong! What is it? I won't let it get to me! I wish I could believe in a god who would comfort me. But, ah…if there were a god, he wouldn't allow his creation to suffer like this. He'd be able to do anything he wished. Most of his creatures are in a miserable state and are anything but happy. Therefore, even if there is a god, he lacks either goodness or power or both. I find no facts to support his existence in my life!

"Perhaps I should make a Kierkegaardian leap of faith to affirm God in my life. But I don't have the will to believe and enter into that abyss! Besides, where would that lead me? Nowhere. Absolutely nowhere. No, as a matter of fact, it would lead me only to what I believe Heidegger refers to as total awareness of one's being. And when that happens, one only becomes too intensely aware of the decaying of their being. I'm sure that's what I'm sensing now. But what is wrong?

A Fad is self identification between people for status

"They won't be satisfied until I do drugs and go to the house like them. Ah, they all do it because it's the status quo here, but in a few years they'll see that I was right. This is the same thing soldiers have resorted to for comfort in other wars. But what good does that do me now? Surely I can find a way out of this abyss I have sunk into! Ah, yes. My friend. My very good friend Sartre said one must affirm himself.

"Even if I can't totally resolve this situation, I'll have to accept it and proclaim it as my finest hour, no matter how fragile my decision may appear. I must affirm my selfhood, assume my own attitudes and take responsibility for what I do. Therefore I, Dan Semple, right or wrong, affirm that I am a pundit, even an elitist! I'll continue to proclaim my beliefs to the bitter end. Most of all, if I leave this place alive, I won't have to be ashamed for compromising my principles. But is it enough?

"Yes! I am right. I've won once more. I can go back to them now." He said defiantly.

*I think
therefore
I am
an ATHEIST*

Computer War fare

* Pencil Neck
Hiding Behind
A Line

It is a pencil neck war.

*If the good Lord ever
screwed-up making a man —
he sure screwed-up there.*

~ ~ ~ ~ ~

Tim: "Shit, man! This place is a hole. Mother Fucker! I thought I'd lived in some slums back home but they weren't anything like this. But I guess it hasn't been all bad. I guess one of the best people I ever met is that honky Bill Freeze.

"I think he wishes he was Black like me 'cause he knows that honkies don't have any soul. No sir. Ain't no way. Blacks have been hurt. We sing it in our songs, the way we walk, the way we dig speaking Bo jive. Shit man, no honky is like us.

"You know, I got just a little more than three months left in this hellhole. Then I'll be home with Annie, and I'm going to bring the max on that bitch, again and again! Yes, sir! We'll do it to death! I love her even if I do call her my bitch. She knows I don't mean anything by it. Aw sure, we play funny games with each other. But we don't really harm each other. You know, one day I'll tell her how much I love her, but not too soon. I'll wait until we get old and gray. I have to keep her guessing until then."

Suddenly he found himself on his knees. "Oh, sweet Jesus, I am saved by your grace, 'cause it's sure as hell I can't do it alone. I did everything over here I wanted to avoid. I just can't help myself, so I'm depending on you to help me now."

Through his tears, he pondered. "Oh, dear Lord Jesus, if I had one last wish, it would be that I could be with Annie one more time. Oh, I love my children, but I could never love them like I do my Annie."

His tears were flowing steadily now. "Annie, I love you. Lord if I die before tonight, take care of her. I love her, Lord…You know, Lord."

He continued almost in shame and looked up to heaven. "I can't separate my love for Annie and my love for you. But, you know, somehow I feel it's almost the same."

Smiling, thinking about Annie, he returned to get high and crazy with the others.

~ ~ ~ ~ ~

Bobby had a warm can of beer in one hand and a joint in the other as he sat away from the others.

"I hate this mother fucking place. It scares the hell out of me. We're going to get hit hard tonight. I know it. Oh, the planes bombed Chuck's ass all day, but I don't think it did any good. Chuck is too smart for that. He's dug too deep in the ground to have a few bombs get to him. Oh well, fuck it. I ain't going to be scared. Even if I was, I wouldn't let anybody know it. No sir, if I'm going to die, I am going to die like a man! Time for another beer.

"I know a lot of other guys are afraid of me because they think I'm crazy. Some even think I'm a murderer. Well, that's all right, I guess, because I think they're a bunch of pussies! Some of them go around thinking they're better than the rest of us. Well, I think they're a bunch of fucking hypocrites. At least everyone knows where I stand. I call 'em like I see 'em. It doesn't matter anyway. None of them can imagine the strength I feel inside since I've come to Vietnam. Maybe I am crazy but I like it here most of the time. Except I'll never get used to being treated as an equal with niggers, wetbacks, and slant eyes! Once I get back home, I'll be able to avoid them altogether. Even the stupid ones know not to come to the land of the stompers in West Texas. 'Cause we'll stomp their fucking asses if we catch them in West Texas after sundown.

"Well, Bobby, it looks like you've come to the end of a long line of fantastic fucks. I had the best reputation back home. No one, and I mean no one, could beat me at drinking, screwing and fighting. Time for another beer.

"I want to make a toast to all those wonderful ladies I shared great times with, and also to all those I missed or I'm gonna miss. Here's to all of you. Thanks. Now, here's to me. The best of the good old boys. I won't let all of the good old boys down now—especially my Dad. He's the best of them.

"Bobby, you are a man." He leaned back on a sandbag and swallowed the beer left in the can. "And I wouldn't let you be anything else. Yeah, a man! I'll drink to that. Come on, you fucking gooks."

He stood and beat his chest. "Chuck, you ain't seen nothing yet. 'Cause we're gonna wipe your ass, even if I have to do it all myself."

Then he started laughing uncontrollably in a high-pitched voice and looked up. "Come on and get me if you want me! 'Cause when you get me, you'll get a real man. There's no stopping Bobby Swenson now."

He ripped opened another can of beer. "Here's another toast to every wild man that ever lived. 'Cause I am going down fighting, just like they did. Yahoo!"

May a green beret drive a personnel carrier over your poster

MY business

Death is ~~MY business~~

AND

Business is Good.

Yeah, though I walk through the valley of the shadow of death, I fear no evil. 'Cause I'm the meanest mother in the valley.

When I die bury me face down so the whole world can kiss my ass. (& the army.)

May the 1st section drive an M-110 SP up your ass. (SIDEWAYS.)

~ ~ ~ ~ ~

"Well, here we are again, just you and me, God," Bill said. "You know, I don't think I ever realized that life could be so terrible. Am I complaining?" He looked up and smiled. "Wouldn't you?" He smelled his armpits. "I haven't had a shower in over three weeks, only the good old army PTA out—prick, tits and armpits. I'd give anything for a shower with clean water. I'm ready to die here. It'd be a lot easier, don't you think?" He stood and shook his fist. "Ah so help me, one of these days I'm going to tell you exactly what I think about this."

Bill looked up at heaven laughing and tried to make another joke again. But stopped. "I'm lost."

He threw himself violently on some sandbags and started crying, then looked up. "You know what really hurts, Father? Oh, it doesn't bother me that they think that I'm queer because I'm not always running to the whorehouse.

"What really hurts is the fact that no one gives a shit about anyone around here! We can't even show our compassion for each other here where we need each other's support so desperately. Each act of kindness is misinterpreted as some sort of deviant sexual behavior.

"Father, I grew up believing in all those ideals which my parents taught me and I learned at the synagogue. I actually believed that people would admire and respect me if I followed your law. Instead I get brutalized every which way I turn.

"When I arrived in Vietnam I was an innocent young Jewish boy from the suburbs of New York who believed deeply in his faith and heritage. I grew up in an insular world and was presumptuous about my faith. I truly believed that no one could know you, Father, like a Jew! I was wrong. You truly are the universal God. Tonight I don't want to get maimed. I'm more afraid of that than dying. Chuck is going to run us over tonight. I can feel it. All of us can. I wonder what the others are thinking. You are in all of them, if they wouldn't deny you. How can anyone ignore you, especially now?

"We're trapped here and have no place to escape. I suppose Flower Power was right that we're all faggots. It's not only due to Vietnam but it's because we're cut off from the God of all creation. Every last one of us has compromised ourselves in one way or another here. It's hard to face how depraved we've become. I believe most of us will return home irreparably damaged. How could you allow this to happen? Most of us were essentially okay before we came to Vietnam. No one should have their soul ravaged daily like this!

"And yet, if we don't despair, we can only be better for it. You have left us naked and besieged by our degradation. We must believe that you are the center of creation. Yet we don't entirely understand your love. One has to be tough minded here not to permit all the evil that permeates this place to obliterate our love for you. Even here there is a possibility of experiencing your love. Through all this pain someone can find freedom through your love. Like Abraham, who had to choose you over his son, and then you delivered him through his pain.

"You know what, Father? I just realized something. It's not the man who stands up and says 'I am' who is strong in this world, and then falls into bondage to self or society. He only continues to rebel against you and keeps you locked out from his soul.

"The person who is strong in this world is the one who stands up and says 'I love' in spite of the unbearable circumstances that have been thrown their way. He continues to love and love more freely and his love becomes the greater because of it. If all of us would have the courage to accept your love, we'd be much better off. There is more strength in the act of loving than giving in to the folly of despair. I pray all of us stop rebelling against you, and learn about the power of your love to overcome even a place like Vietnam.

"There is no God but God." He looked up, smiled, gave the peace symbol, and returned to his friends.

Chapter 15: FLARES LIGHT THE NIGHT SKY

Previous wars that the United States was involved in were more about defending a defined piece of real estate. Vietnam is less about defending real estate and more about hunting and killing your enemy.

Dan Semple

SINCE HEARING FROM BATTALION to prepare for a full assault by the enemy, Captain Biddle ordered that flares be shot in the sky every half hour. It was a dark night, darker than any they could remember. The sky was cloudy, blackening the moon and stars, while they were engulfed by the jungle canopy.

Flares were useful for spotting Vietcong or sappers. When they floated from the sky, it was almost as bright as the afternoon. But there was a limited number available so they could only be used every half hour.

Suddenly Renegade was hit with gunfire on all sides of the perimeter. Within the confines of the unit, mortars fell, exploding. All around they were frantically trying to locate an enemy they couldn't see, trying to defend themselves.

On all sides of the perimeter, men were busy responding to the onslaught of mortar shells. They shot their weapons into the dark without knowing if they were hitting anything. Their best hope for survival was to keep Chuck from penetrating the perimeter. Some of the members of A Battery who had never fought in direct combat were assigned to defensive positions on the perimeter.

At the edge of the encampment, Dan had been assigned to watch the perimeter next to Bobby. Before the attack, Bobby gave Dan careful instructions on what he should look for.

"Bobby, I'm glad I'm with you if anything happens. It gives me some confidence that I might live through this. I think you know more about surviving an enemy attack than anyone in the unit, including the captain and the first sergeant. I don't mind telling you I've never been so fucking scared in my life."

"Well, this is a helluva fucking way to get indoctrinated, boy. Don't worry about it. We'll be fine. Our primary job is to kill as many gooks as possible." Bobby smiled, delighted that Dan had acknowledged him and his reputation.

"I never thought I'd hear myself say this, but I think it's better that one of them die than me. I'm ready to do whatever I have to do to get the hell home," Dan responded.

Bobby was surprised to hear this. "I know," he said quietly. "All of us feel that way when we're confronted with any enemy we know wants to kill us before we kill them. You know the old saying. Kill or be killed." Bobby nodded. Dan shook his head yes. "Besides, you and I are almost short. I don't want to fuck that up for anyone."

They did not speak another word until the attack. When they received incoming rounds, Dan followed Bobby's lead and fired when he fired. It frustrated Dan that he couldn't see any sappers, who blended in so well into the night terrain. But after watching Bobby in action he began to understand what to do.

As a flare floated down in the sky, Dan noticed what appeared to be a tiny flap of a black loincloth blowing in the breeze. He concentrated on the area and eventually saw the outline of a sapper's body. He was lying quietly just twenty feet in front of them.

Dan began firing several times. He saw the jerky movements of the sapper's arms flapping in the air. The man was gasping for breath. Dan had hit him in the chest. Then the incendiary grenade that he was carrying exploded.

Dan was surprised to be proud for a moment. He had killed one of the enemy.

"Fuck him," Dan thought. "Who knows how many Americans he may have got with the grenades he had for A Battery?"

Bobby was still next to Dan. He noticed what Dan had just accomplished. He did not say a word but patted him on the back as they lay in the dirt peering over sandbags. Then he continued firing without any interruption.

At that time, Bobby's approval meant more to Dan than he could ever express. "I finally have earned my manhood," he thought. "I can look at my father or any other man in the eyes and not be ashamed. Now I measure up. I killed someone on the battlefield."

He was not concerned with any pietistic notions. He would consider the impact another time. Now he was fighting to save as many lives in the unit as he could. He was firing his weapon with Bobby at anything that moved, or just into the still darkness.

After an hour the mortars and the incoming sappers stopped. No one left their assigned position. Tense and scared, they braced themselves for another attack. But the enemy they could not see didn't come. The soldiers knew that A Battery would be attacked. They just didn't know when.

"Only Chuck knows when and how this will happen," Bobby told Dan as they scanned through the darkness.

~ ~ ~ ~ ~

For two hours it was overwhelmingly quiet. The stillness was more difficult to deal with than the combat. At exactly 2330 hours the enemy started firing on A Battery's northern perimeter. The men there returned fire without any targets. But on the other three sides it was total calm. They waited for Chuck to attack. No one knew how to respond because they didn't know where Chuck was going to hit next.

Then every few minutes mortars exploded at different parts of the perimeter, randomly hitting different sections.

Several flares flew up. They had to see if there were any sappers at the perimeter. Then squads of snipers started firing at A Battery in rotation. The snipers were high in the trees, placed strategically by Chuck so the American soldiers would be easy targets. The flares were supposed to protect the Americans but now they were employed by the enemy snipers to kill them.

In a short time several men in A Battery were killed or wounded. Orders went out not to fire flares until everyone was camouflaged from the enemy. In the dark the sappers could penetrate the perimeter. When there were no flares in the sky, the sappers entered the unit. There was chaos. Everyone survived on instincts and fear.

Bill and the new recruit Blondie were next to each other, lying on the ground with a few sandbags in front of them for protection.

Blondie seemed like a nice kid.

"He's obviously so scared he's paralyzed with fear," Bill thought, sensing him glance around panicked whenever Bill fired into the darkness. "He simply doesn't know how to respond. His military training hasn't prepared him for this. Now he knows that the only way to learn to defend yourself in combat is through on-the-job training. It's too late now."

He wished there was something that he could say. Hours earlier, he had told Blondie that everything would be okay and that many of them had been through something like this lots of times. This was not true, but Bill's encouragement had seemed to give Blondie the confidence he needed to begin fighting back.

Suddenly Bill heard the sound of a bullet fly close to him. He felt Blondie's limp body fall on him. Blondie was hit in the neck.

"He's over now. He won't survive the hit," Bill thought, startled.

"Blondie, you'll be okay," he said gently. "I'll hold you until the medic comes."

Blondie knew he was dying rapidly. He looked at Bill and said, "Please tell my family that I love them."

"Yes," Bill said quietly.

"Thank you."

That was when Bill realized that he didn't even know Blondie's name. All he knew was that Blondie was eighteen years old and from a small town in Pennsylvania. Bill became angrier than he had ever been in his life.

"Why did someone so young have to die?"

He grabbed his weapon and began firing methodically, more focused on killing the enemy than ever before. He spied a sapper and waited for him to get close enough so he could kill him with his bare hands.

Bill jumped the sapper unexpectedly, stabbed him with his knife, cut off his head and watched the body convulse itself to death. He threw the sapper's head back to the jungle at Chuck.

"To give you a warning of what to expect," Bill muttered crazily, enraged. He did not calm down until after the attack was over. Once there was a lull in the combat he realized what had happened, but he felt no remorse.

"Fuck him. I'm going to kill any other gook that comes into the confines of the unit. I am going to kill every last one of the mother fuckers in memory of my best friend Chris and Blondie!"

He wondered now if this wasn't why he had wanted to come to Vietnam from the beginning. He would never have admitted it before.

"Nothing will stop me. There's no time here to consider the right or wrong of this shit. I gotta defend the men in this unit. Unless I'm willing to play the part, someone else in A Battery will die. Fuck 'em. Bring on Chuck. I'm ready!" He waited for the next movement, for the next thing to shoot at.

~ ~ ~ ~ ~

Exhausted and overcome with fear, they had been waiting three and a half hours. It was now 0338 hours. A Battery was hoping that Chuck was going to leave them alone the rest of the night. Everyone wired on combat. No one could sleep.

Captain Biddle had been moving from section to section throughout the night. He was with the Commo Section and talking to Tim. It was the first time Tim had had the opportunity to have a conversation with him. Between taking and sending orders, they shared about their wives and their children and how much they missed them.

"The captain is just like me. We both just want what is best for our families," Tim reflected. He had respected Biddle as an officer before, but now he admired the man's compassion. Captain Biddle gave the Commo Section confidence.

Again, machine guns and snipers started firing into the perimeter of the unit. The Northern Vietcong fighters were more accurate than the Cong in South Vietnam. The bombing was sporadic this time. Commo Section could not decipher any pattern. They had no alternative but to fire in the dark, hoping it would do something to deter Chuck.

Peeking over their sandbag walls, the men in Commo Section saw a sapper sneaking inside the perimeter loaded with grenades. It had taken Chuck seven and a half hours to accomplish this. The whole unit was in danger now.

Captain Biddle saw him first and shot him with his pistol. Before collapsing, the sapper threw a grenade into their sandbag box. Without hesitation, Biddle threw his body on the grenade.

Tim watched the captain's body fly into the air. When he ran over and found him dead, he was shocked.

"One of the finest men I've ever known saved my life," Tim thought crying. "This white guy saved me? With prejudice towards almost every honky, I can never say thank you enough. But maybe I can..." He was not aware how much he hated most whites until now.

Immediately Tim went to tell Long what had happened to Captain Biddle. The hardened war veteran burst out crying and asked Tim to take him to see the captain's body.

"Why couldn't it have been an old son-of-a-bitch like me?" the first sergeant said through his tears when they came to Biddle's body. "He had so much to live for. He was the finest officer I've ever served under." No one else could say anything.

~ ~ ~ ~ ~

When morning arrived, there were four dead and thirteen wounded. Three of them were hurt enough to be airlifted along with the dead. Those three did not want to be taken away. They knew A Battery still had to defend LZ Renegade.

Early in the morning, orders came from Battalion to blow up the big guns, the ammunition, and anything that was mobilized by tracks. All the vehicles on tracks were bogged down in the mud. None of them would be fully mobile until the rainy season ended.

To get out of the jungle quickly, A Battery had to destroy everything, so that Chuck could not use it. It took only a few hours to dismantle and blow up everything.

"Hopefully, there ain't nothing left for Chuck to claim," Long said.

The unit moved out. As they headed back, U.S. Air Force planes bombed both sides of the road to protect A Battery as much as possible. Smoke rose from the jungle around them. As they retreated from LZ Renegade, they looked back at the devastation they had left behind. The ground was burnt, and the jungle was scorched around the perimeter.

It was sad to move out from that place. So many of the men had lost their lives there. Leaving it meant they were saying their final farewell to the dead. They had defended this area for less than three weeks, and now the Vietcong would reclaim it.

First Sergeant Long pondered this as he rode in the lead vehicle.

"What the hell was this combat all about? Have we accomplished nothing? When all is said and done, I know Chuck can claim the victory for this nameless battle. We fought so valiantly last night. So what?"

You are here to serve. Not fight for freedom.

The sound I will always hate is the sound of a bullet that misses you and hits your friend.

I think I will always remember the good times in Vietnam. I think there may have been 2 or 3?

365 DAYS
and a WAKE UP!!

Blondie, I'm sorry we forgot to learn your name.

Chapter 16: GOING HOME

THE DAY ARRIVED for Bill, Dan, Tim and Bobby to return home. It was hard to believe. "The nightmare is almost over," Bill said to Dan over breakfast that morning.

Three and a half months had passed quickly. They had had a few minor skirmishes with the Vietcong at their old base camp, but none was like LZ Renegade.

"After that night, I became totally anesthetized to the pain here," Dan replied. "Will I ever have the strength to feel anything again? I don't know."

Their uneventful departure from the unit filled them with agony.

"I'm a traitor leaving the others behind," Bill said. "No matter what I've experienced, it's become their home now, and we're leaving less experienced soldiers to defend themselves."

"I can't help wondering why I didn't die," Dan asked sipping his coffee. "In our time at A Battery we've seen men die and even more wounded."

"It's not comforting to know that our survival was a matter of chance. Hell, it certainly was not the survival of the fittest. I accept, though it's hard to, that we were absolutely powerless in determining whether we'd live or die."

Dan leaned back in his chair. "I've seen other combat vets from previous wars. This is something they grapple with. They mature and have a more objective perspective. None of them process the impact of their experiences while it was happening, because everything moved too fast for them. Vietnam will slowly reveal itself to them—to us—in unexpected ways back in the world. For me, I'm done. I'm ready to walk away and forget it."

"Me too," Bill replied. They sat in silence for a long time.

Each had made plans for the future. They had established goals. It gave them a sense of security. They were once more in control of their lives.

Bill thought about that. He watched Dan eat his breakfast. He watched the other soldiers in the mess tent. "Will they ever be able to forgive themselves? Will they ever be able to forgive God for allowing this to happen? Or perhaps there is even less reason to believe in God after this experience? Time will tell whether they'll be able to transcend the desolation that they've experienced. I've been here for the past twelve months. It's a blessing that they have no idea how Vietnam will deter them from fulfilling their dreams, from having a future."

Bobby, like Sergeant Chen, had decided to reenlist and extend his tour of duty in Vietnam for another twelve months. When he returned from leave, he would take Chen's place as Section Chief for Gun Section #1. On that day he was very excited about going home. He had received a letter from his dad. On his return the town would give him a war hero's welcome.

He remained a hawk, but he had not come to terms with the way the U.S. Army operated in Vietnam. This did not affect his decision to reenlist. He wanted to win.

Annie and Tim's two children would be waiting for Tim at the airport. They would be the only people he wanted to see when he arrived. He had a blue-collar job waiting for him at the factory where had enjoyed working at in the past.

In Vietnam he had read Ralph Ellison's book *Invisible Man* at the encouragement of Dan and Bill. He had decided to go to college and use his Veterans Benefits. Annie was very excited. They would be moving to Atlanta.

Tim had probationary acceptance at Emory University but had to pass the GED before being fully accepted. He was thankful for his friendship with Dan and Bill that had grown to mean so much to him. His worldview had been broadened through their influence.

Since the combat at LZ Renegade, Dan had taken the time to examine his life and had developed a new perspective. He wrote to his parents to let them know how much he loved them. His mother wept with joy when she received her letter. It was like listening to the Dan she knew before he had become estranged from her. His father was excited too. Dan told him he planned on working fulltime at the family business, beginning after he earned an MBA from Stanford University.

His heart had opened to a potential relationship with Cathy. In the last letter he wrote to her he said he was falling in love. He wanted to see how their relationship would grow after he returned home. He knew she could be the woman he married. Cathy wrote him consistently during his tour of duty and mailed him packages of books. It helped him keep a portion of his sanity. He owed her more than he could say and hoped to tell her one day.

Bill wanted to see his family and friends. He knew that the first thing he was going to do was to pick up his little brother and hold him tight. He was going to tell Adam that he had kept his promise about coming home because he loved him. Then he was going to give him a kiss on his forehead.

He wanted to go back to college, but he thought about a job close to home so he could be with his family and friends for a while. He grew to appreciate them more than ever. He considered growing his hair long, letting his beard grow, and backpacking through Europe. It was something he had talked about doing with his best friend Chris the summer of their senior year of high school. But Chris had left for the U.S. Army right after graduation so there was no time to fulfill their dream. Chris had died in Vietnam two years ago, which was why Bill had signed up to go. Now he would do it for both of them with the money he had saved. But he had never made up his mind whether it was the right choice to go to Vietnam.

~ ~ ~ ~ ~

They were scheduled to leave around 0900 hours, riding along with some other men on ammo run, catching a noon flight from Phu Cat Air Force Base to Cam Ranh Bay. Before they left, Bill decided to visit the Bitch Wall one last time.

No one else was around. He took his time to examine the wall without any interruption. He remembered when each thought was written and knew the author in most cases. The wall told A Battery's story. Most of the comments made him smile, a few brought tears. But most of all, they filled his heart with pride about what they had accomplished together.

"I remember the night we created the Bitch Wall, when Flower Power and Phil Caldwell argued over what to call it," he said to himself.

"You were right, Flower Power. The title explains best who we were in Vietnam. You made so many things clear for the rest of us. I remember your best friend Phil Caldwell drawing the beautiful woman in the bikini. I don't know for sure but I bet his girlfriend back home has red hair, because I know she was Irish. I'm sure Phil and I would have visited each other if he had lived."

He thought about Flower Power and Phil in New York City. He imagined meeting in diners and talking on the subway. He pictured the three of them marching in a war protest.

"I remember watching with envy as all of you inhaled the evil weed. I didn't have the courage to let myself go like you, because I was afraid of what I might do and regret it. Now I wish I had smoked a little of it with you."

Your Mind is a Kalidascope
Our bunker runneth over

LSD

Freak Out

and break
through to
the other
side.

ACID HEAD

"When they were high, I remember what everyone enjoyed talking about the most was the girls back home. I think that kept us sane more than anything else we could have done."

The girls back home are a
scare comodity. Accidents cause
People.

Climax

"For me it was not a girl back home but a wonderful woman I met in Australia. I'll be writing her when I return home. This is a promise I must keep."

Wendy

"The very thought of her and my times with her have kept me from losing contact with who I was before I came to Vietnam. I guess I'm no different than Tim, because it was the love of a woman that helped save me. There's so much else here, but I think the core to everything is love. No matter how crude or how eloquent, it's about love."

LOVE

Bill took one final long look at the wall in its entirety. It took his breath away. He thought, "What we have said together, none of us could have said alone."

He decided he had to add one more thing on the wall before he left A Battery for good. He grabbed a red marker and wrote

Escaped to NYC!
-B.F.

"That says it all."

Bill thought that in the next couple of months most of the men in A Battery would not even know who B.F. was, but he was sure they'd continue their story on the wall. It was 0845 hours. He heard Dan and Tim calling him in the distance to come down and load on the truck. They wanted to head home.

As they rode in the back of the truck, Bill admired the Vietnam countryside one last time. He still found it picturesque but it held no magic anymore. It was not like the first time he had seen it. He thought, "Behind that beauty lies a darkness that I hope I'll never experience again."

~ ~ ~ ~ ~

At the airport at Cam Ranh Bay they found themselves waiting anxiously for the freedom bird to take them home. They waited with men who had served in the same police action. Most of them had experienced little or no combat. Others had suffered much more than the men did in A Battery.

Bill and Dan continued their conversation from the mess tent that morning.

"I can't believe I'm here," Dan said to Bill. "Look at all these guys going home."

"But look around," Bill replied. "Everyone is leaving Vietnam irrecoverably damaged. Look at them." He didn't look at Dan but stared way out at a point somewhere in the wide open airfield.

The four of them knew each other better than most people. Few words were exchanged. They did not have the courage to look each other in the eyes. If they did, they would find deep-seated guilt and shame that only they would understand.

"I'd prefer that no one else knows what we've experienced, especially our family and friends back home," Bill thought. "Even though I'm petrified about what lies ahead, it no longer makes any difference what anyone succumbed to in Vietnam. At all costs we'll defend each other since no one else will understand back home. We've become accustomed to an unreality that is totally estranged from the secure reality that exists in America, which we'll soon be reentering."

It was the exact same spot as twelve months earlier on their flight to Vietnam. Once they arrived at Fort Lewis, they would be home in less than twenty-four hours.

"The transition returning home is going to be more difficult than our adjustment to Vietnam," Bill thought. "I now operate by standards not acceptable back home. Will I lose control? Will I become another statistic like so many other vets, because I'll be rejected for having served in Vietnam? I can be the convenient scapegoat for everyone."

We shall cease
from exploring,
and at the end
of our exploration,
we return to where
we started, and
know the place for
the first time.
                    T.S. Elliot

They boarded the luxury airliner for Fort Lewis. The stewardesses watched the returning soldiers enter the plane. They wondered what had happened to these men that had caused so many to become sullen and lifeless.

The stewardesses were on guard during the return flight home. They had seen men fall apart. It was not uncommon. They were afraid of becoming war trophies too.

"Who can blame them under the circumstances? Round eyed women…" Bill thought over a Budweiser.

The stewardesses felt compelled to be efficient but avoided getting too close to the men hiding underneath the despair. They wondered if anyone would ever have the courage to openly listen to them without harshly judging.

The twenty hour flight from Cam Ranh Bay included a two-hour layover in Tokyo for refueling, but they were not allowed to get off the plane while it was being refueled.

Their trip went faster than anticipated. Most of the men slept almost the entire flight to Tacoma. It had been the first time in a year they felt finally relaxed enough to fall into a deep sleep. Less than forty-eight hours since Bill, Dan, Tim and Bobby left A Battery, they arrived at Fort Lewis. Most of them would be home with their families in less than another twenty-four hours.

The lights were turned on, startling them. They woke from their sleep. Then without warning a stewardess got on a loud speaker. "Please prepare for the landing in Tacoma… Let's count. All together now 10…9…8…7…6…5…4…3…2…1 HOORAY!"

ABOUT THE AUTHOR

Dennis Lane

Like most Vietnam War veterans, Lane continues to struggle with PTSD and has been reticent about sharing his experience with others. He volunteered for the draft and served in Vietnam with a combat unit for 14 ½ months, earning an Army Commendation Medal. He also served as Catholic missionary in Orange Walk Town, Belize, Central America for two years. The combination of these two experiences transformed his life. While he considers himself a Christian, he embraces people of other faiths and atheists. He is known by everyone as being the least judgmental person they know.

His missionary and combat experiences influenced him so much that he entered the Jesuit Seminary. After 1½ years he

determined that it was too confining and left. He has earned a
BA in English with three minors in Spanish, Communication,
and Theology. Later he earned Masters' Degrees in Math,
and Economics. He started Ph.D. in Economics but never
completed it and has no regrets. While studying in
Washington, D.C. during President Jimmy Carter's
administration, he worked on the President's Commission on
Federal Impact Aid as a staff economist.

Today Lane continues to serve the disenfranchised by
working at inner-city social service/healthcare organizations.
He is an active community volunteer and remains involved in
the Roman Catholic Church. He has taught 4th and 5th
Graders Bible Study for over 23 years. He maintains an
active social life with friends and family. His passion to serve
others seems unlimited. However, he considers himself a
"Cafeteria Catholic" — he picks and chooses what he
believes is true. Like most American Catholics, he does not
depend on the Pope to determine "absolute truth."

Lane is a world traveler and delights in becoming
immersed in different cultures. This has given him an insight
that has proved invaluable to him in his personal and
professional lives. He is very gregarious and outgoing. What
earmarks him is his unbridled love and passion for others. He
prefers living alone with his best friend, Clifford the Cat. He
is very much a free spirit and is always excited about what
the world has waiting for him. He has maintained his
childlike enthusiasm throughout his life, not giving in to
despair. He believes his life remains in balance because he
has always worked out 3 — 5 times a week and attempts to
eat organically as much as possible. He is not a vegetarian;
the meat he eats is hormone- and antibiotic-free.

He has written many news articles, fundraising letters, and
grants for the inner-city organizations that he continues to
serve.

People will find his approach unique, fresh, and
uncomplicated.

THE BITCH WALL LIVES!

Please feel free to write your thoughts. I encourage people to write their thoughts in the back of this book or on my website.

www.vietnamwailingwall.com

~   ~   ~   ~   ~

Facing Death, Facing Faith

Days when God is a spinning compass,
chewing cigarettes as your last meal
trying to remember what it's like
to feel something besides fear.
The death of ambiguity,
Lying in the marshy thickness
of guns and bombs,
lost in the friendship of sacrifice.
There is pain within pain.
Days when God is a mortal wound,
a friend's blood soaked hand,
and the instinct to crawl into the
deepest hole you can find.
All you can do is rest in the misery
but know that what you are is only
a tiny part of a larger whole.
God created tears for a reason
and graffiti the comic grace
where suffering and art collide.

David Blanton
Street Poet
October 25, 2014
New Orleans, LA

RAMBLE HOUSE's

HARRY STEPHEN KEELER WEBWORK MYSTERIES

(RH) indicates the title is available ONLY in the RAMBLE HOUSE edition

The Ace of Spades Murder
The Affair of the Bottled Deuce (RH)
The Amazing Web
The Barking Clock
Behind That Mask
The Book with the Orange Leaves
The Bottle with the Green Wax Seal
The Box from Japan
The Case of the Canny Killer
The Case of the Crazy Corpse (RH)
The Case of the Flying Hands (RH)
The Case of the Ivory Arrow
The Case of the Jeweled Ragpicker
The Case of the Lavender Gripsack
The Case of the Mysterious Moll
The Case of the 16 Beans
The Case of the Transparent Nude (RH)
The Case of the Transposed Legs
The Case of the Two-Headed Idiot (RH)
The Case of the Two Strange Ladies
The Circus Stealers (RH)
Cleopatra's Tears
A Copy of Beowulf (RH)
The Crimson Cube (RH)
The Face of the Man From Saturn
Find the Clock
The Five Silver Buddhas
The 4th King
The Gallows Waits, My Lord! (RH)
The Green Jade Hand
Finger! Finger!
Hangman's Nights (RH)
I, Chameleon (RH)
I Killed Lincoln at 10:13! (RH)
The Iron Ring
The Man Who Changed His Skin (RH)
The Man with the Crimson Box
The Man with the Magic Eardrums
The Man with the Wooden Spectacles
The Marceau Case
The Matilda Hunter Murder

The Monocled Monster
The Murder of London Lew
The Murdered Mathematician
The Mysterious Card (RH)
The Mysterious Ivory Ball of Wong Shing Li (RH)
The Mystery of the Fiddling Cracksman
The Peacock Fan
The Photo of Lady X (RH)
The Portrait of Jirjohn Cobb
Report on Vanessa Hewstone (RH)
Riddle of the Travelling Skull
Riddle of the Wooden Parrakeet (RH)
The Scarlet Mummy (RH)
The Search for X-Y-Z
The Sharkskin Book
Sing Sing Nights
The Six From Nowhere (RH)
The Skull of the Waltzing Clown
The Spectacles of Mr. Cagliostro
Stand By—London Calling!
The Steeltown Strangler
The Stolen Gravestone (RH)
Strange Journey (RH)
The Strange Will
The Straw Hat Murders (RH)
The Street of 1000 Eyes (RH)
Thieves' Nights
Three Novellos (RH)
The Tiger Snake
The Trap (RH)
Vagabond Nights (Defrauded Yeggman)
Vagabond Nights 2 (10 Hours)
The Vanishing Gold Truck
The Voice of the Seven Sparrows
The Washington Square Enigma
When Thief Meets Thief
The White Circle (RH)
The Wonderful Scheme of Mr. Christopher Thorne
X. Jones—of Scotland Yard
Y. Cheung, Business Detective

Keeler Related Works

A To Izzard: A Harry Stephen Keeler Companion by Fender Tucker — Articles and stories about Harry, by Harry, and in his style. Included is a compleat bibliography.

Wild About Harry: Reviews of Keeler Novels — Edited by Richard Polt & Fender Tucker — 22 reviews of works by Harry Stephen Keeler from *Keeler News*. A perfect introduction to the author.

The Keeler Keyhole Collection: Annotated newsletter rants from Harry Stephen Keeler, edited by Francis M. Nevins. Over 400 pages of incredibly personal Keeleriana.

Fakealoo — Pastiches of the style of Harry Stephen Keeler by selected demented members of the HSK Society. Updated every year with the new winner.

Strands of the Web: Short Stories of Harry Stephen Keeler — 29 stories, just about all that Keeler wrote, are edited and introduced by Fred Cleaver.

RAMBLE HOUSE's Loon Sanctuary

A Clear Path to Cross — Sharon Knowles short mystery stories by Ed Lynskey.

A Corpse Walks in Brooklyn and Other Stories — Volume 5 in the Day Keene in the Detective Pulps series.

A Jimmy Starr Omnibus — Three 40s novels by Jimmy Starr.

A Niche in Time and Other Stories — Classic SF by William F. Temple

A Roland Daniel Double: The Signal and The Return of Wu Fang — Classic thrillers from the 30s.

A Shot Rang Out — Three decades of reviews and articles by today's Anthony Boucher, Jon Breen. An essential book for any mystery lover's library.

A Smell of Smoke — A 1951 English countryside thriller by Miles Burton.

A Snark Selection — Lewis Carroll's *The Hunting of the Snark* with two Snarkian chapters by Harry Stephen Keeler — Illustrated by Gavin L. O'Keefe.

A Young Man's Heart — A forgotten early classic by Cornell Woolrich.

Alexander Laing Novels — *The Motives of Nicholas Holtz* and *Dr. Scarlett*, stories of medical mayhem and intrigue from the 30s.

An Angel in the Street — Modern hardboiled noir by Peter Genovese.

Automaton — Brilliant treatise on robotics: 1928-style! By H. Stafford Hatfield.

Away From the Here and Now — Clare Winger Harris stories, collected by Richard A. Lupoff

Beast or Man? — A 1930 novel of racism and horror by Sean M'Guire. Introduced by John Pelan.

Black Beadle — A 1939 thriller by E.C.R. Lorac.

Black Hogan Strikes Again — Australia's Peter Renwick pens a tale of the 30s outback.

Black River Falls — Suspense from the master, Ed Gorman.

Blondy's Boy Friend — A snappy 1930 story by Philip Wylie, writing as Leatrice Homesley.

Blood in a Snap — The *Finnegan's Wake* of the 21st century, by Jim Weiler.

Blood Moon — The first of the Robert Payne series by Ed Gorman.

Bogart '48 — Hollywood action with Bogie by John Stanley and Kenn Davis

Calling Lou Largo! — Two Lou Largo novels by William Ard.

Cornucopia of Crime — Francis M. Nevins assembled this huge collection of his writings about crime literature and the people who write it. Essential for any serious mystery library.

Corpse Without Flesh — Strange novel of forensics by George Bruce

Crimson Clown Novels — By Johnston McCulley, author of the Zorro novels, *The Crimson Clown* and *The Crimson Clown Again*.

Dago Red — 22 tales of dark suspense by Bill Pronzini.

Dark Sanctuary — Weird Menace story by H. B. Gregory

David Hume Novels — *Corpses Never Argue, Cemetery First Stop, Make Way for the Mourners, Eternity Here I Come*. 1930s British hardboiled fiction with an attitude.

Dead Man Talks Too Much — Hollywood boozer by Weed Dickenson.

Death Leaves No Card — One of the most unusual murdered-in-the-tub mysteries you'll ever read. By Miles Burton.

Death March of the Dancing Dolls and Other Stories — Volume Three in the Day Keene in the Detective Pulps series. Introduced by Bill Crider.

Deep Space and other Stories — A collection of SF gems by Richard A. Lupoff.

Detective Duff Unravels It — Episodic mysteries by Harvey O'Higgins.

Diabolic Candelabra — Classic 30s mystery by E.R. Punshon

Dictator's Way — Another D.S. Bobby Owen mystery from E.R. Punshon

Dime Novels: Ramble House's 10-Cent Books — *Knife in the Dark* by Robert Leslie Bellem, *Hot Lead* and *Song of Death* by Ed Earl Repp, *A Hashish House in New York* by H.H. Kane, and five more.

Doctor Arnoldi — Tiffany Thayer's story of the death of death.

Don Diablo: Book of a Lost Film — Two-volume treatment of a western by Paul Landres, with diagrams. Intro by Francis M. Nevins.

Dope and Swastikas — Two strange novels from 1922 by Edmund Snell

Dope Tales #1 — Two dope-riddled classics; *Dope Runners* by Gerald Grantham and *Death Takes the Joystick* by Phillip Condé.

Dope Tales #2 — Two more narco-classics; *The Invisible Hand* by Rex Dark and *The Smokers of Hashish* by Norman Berrow.

Dope Tales #3 — Two enchanting novels of opium by the master, Sax Rohmer. *Dope* and *The Yellow Claw.*

Double Hot — Two 60s softcore sex novels by Morris Hershman.

Double Sex — Yet two more panting thrillers from Morris Hershman.

Dr. Odin — Douglas Newton's 1933 racial potboiler comes back to life.

Evangelical Cockroach — Jack Woodford writes about writing.

Evidence in Blue — 1938 mystery by E. Charles Vivian.

Fatal Accident — Murder by automobile, a 1936 mystery by Cecil M. Wills.

Fighting Mad — Todd Robbins' 1922 novel about boxing and life

Finger-prints Never Lie — A 1939 classic detective novel by John G. Brandon.

Freaks and Fantasies — Eerie tales by Tod Robbins, collaborator of Tod Browning on the film FREAKS.

Gadsby — A lipogram (a novel without the letter E). Ernest Vincent Wright's last work, published in 1939 right before his death.

Gelett Burgess Novels — *The Master of Mysteries, The White Cat, Two O'Clock Courage, Ladies in Boxes, Find the Woman, The Heart Line, The Picaroons* and *Lady Mechante.* Recently added is A Gelett Burgess Sampler, edited by Alfred Jan. All are introduced by Richard A. Lupoff.

Geronimo — S. M. Barrett's 1905 autobiography of a noble American.

Hake Talbot Novels — *Rim of the Pit, The Hangman's Handyman.* Classic locked room mysteries, with mapback covers by Gavin O'Keefe.

Hands Out of Hell and Other Stories — John H. Knox's eerie hallucinations

Hell is a City — William Ard's masterpiece.

Hollywood Dreams — A novel of Tinsel Town and the Depression by Richard O'Brien.

Hostesses in Hell and Other Stories — Russell Gray's most graphic stories

House of the Restless Dead — Strange and ominous tales by Hugh B. Cave.

I Stole $16,000,000 — A true story by cracksman Herbert E. Wilson.

Inclination to Murder — 1966 thriller by New Zealand's Harriet Hunter.

Invaders from the Dark — Classic werewolf tale from Greye La Spina.

J. Poindexter, Colored — Classic satirical black novel by Irvin S. Cobb.

Jack Mann Novels — Strange murder in the English countryside. *Gees' First Case, Nightmare Farm, Grey Shapes, The Ninth Life, The Glass Too Many, Her Ways Are Death, The Kleinert Case* and *Maker of Shadows.*

Jake Hardy — A lusty western tale from Wesley Tallant.

Jim Harmon Double Novels — *Vixen Hollow/Celluloid Scandal, The Man Who Made Maniacs/Silent Siren, Ape Rape/Wanton Witch, Sex Burns Like Fire/Twist Session, Sudden Lust/Passion Strip, Sin Unlimited/Harlot Master, Twilight Girls/Sex Institution.* Written in the early 60s and never reprinted until now.

Joel Townsley Rogers Novels and Short Stories — By the author of *The Red Right Hand: Once In a Red Moon, Lady With the Dice, The Stopped Clock, Never Leave My Bed.* Also two short story collections: *Night of Horror* and *Killing Time.*

John Carstairs, Space Detective — Arboreal Sci-fi by Frank Belknap Long

Joseph Shallit Novels — *The Case of the Billion Dollar Body, Lady Don't Die on My Doorstep, Kiss the Killer, Yell Bloody Murder, Take Your Last Look.* One of America's best 50's authors and a favorite of author Bill Pronzini.

Keller Memento — 45 short stories of the amazing and weird by Dr. David Keller.

Killer's Caress — Cary Moran's 1936 hardboiled thriller.

Lady of the Yellow Death and Other Stories — More stories by Wyatt Blassingame.

League of the Grateful Dead and Other Stories — Volume One in the Day Keene in the Detective Pulps series.

Library of Death — Ghastly tale by Ronald S. L. Harding, introduced by John Pelan

Malcolm Jameson Novels and Short Stories — *Astonishing! Astounding!, Tarnished Bomb, The Alien Envoy and Other Stories* and *The Chariots of San Fernando and Other Stories.* All introduced and edited by John Pelan or Richard A. Lupoff.

Man Out of Hell and Other Stories — Volume II of the John H. Knox weird pulps collection.

Marblehead: A Novel of H.P. Lovecraft — A long-lost masterpiece from Richard A. Lupoff. This is the "director's cut", the long version that has never been published before.

Mark of the Laughing Death and Other Stories — Shockers from the pulps by Francis James, introduced by John Pelan.

Master of Souls — Mark Hansom's 1937 shocker is introduced by weirdologist John Pelan.

Max Afford Novels — *Owl of Darkness, Death's Mannikins, Blood on His Hands, The Dead Are Blind, The Sheep and the Wolves, Sinners in Paradise* and *Two Locked Room Mysteries and a Ripping Yarn* by one of Australia's finest mystery novelists.

Money Brawl — Two books about the writing business by Jack Woodford and H. Bedford-Jones. Introduced by Richard A. Lupoff.

More Secret Adventures of Sherlock Holmes — Gary Lovisi's second collection of tales about the unknown sides of the great detective.

Muddled Mind: Complete Works of Ed Wood, Jr. — David Hayes and Hayden Davis deconstruct the life and works of the mad, but canny, genius.

Murder among the Nudists — A mystery from 1934 by Peter Hunt, featuring a naked Detective-Inspector going undercover in a nudist colony.

Murder in Black and White — 1931 classic tennis whodunit by Evelyn Elder.

Murder in Shawnee — Two novels of the Alleghenies by John Douglas: *Shawnee Alley Fire* and *Haunts.*

Murder in Silk — A 1937 Yellow Peril novel of the silk trade by Ralph Trevor.

My Deadly Angel — 1955 Cold War drama by John Chelton.

My First Time: The One Experience You Never Forget — Michael Birchwood — 64 true first-person narratives of how they lost it.

Mysterious Martin, the Master of Murder — Two versions of a strange 1912 novel by Tod Robbins about a man who writes books that can kill.

Norman Berrow Novels — *The Bishop's Sword, Ghost House, Don't Go Out After Dark, Claws of the Cougar, The Smokers of Hashish, The Secret Dancer, Don't Jump Mr. Boland!, The Footprints of Satan, Fingers for Ransom, The Three Tiers of Fantasy, The Spaniard's Thumb, The Eleventh Plague, Words Have Wings, One Thrilling Night, The Lady's in Danger, It Howls at Night, The Terror in the Fog, Oil Under the Window, Murder in the Melody, The Singing Room.* This is the complete Norman Berrow library of locked-room mysteries, several of which are masterpieces.

Old Faithful and Other Stories — SF classic tales by Raymond Z. Gallun.

Old Times' Sake — Short stories by James Reasoner from Mike Shayne Magazine.

One Dreadful Night — A classic mystery by Ronald S. L. Harding

Pair O' Jacks — A mystery novel and a diatribe about publishing by Jack Woodford

Perfect .38 — Two early Timothy Dane novels by William Ard. More to come.

Prince Pax — Devilish intrigue by George Sylvester Viereck and Philip Eldridge

Prose Bowl — Futuristic satire of a world where hack writing has replaced football as our national obsession, by Bill Pronzini and Barry N. Malzberg.

Red Light — The history of legal prostitution in Shreveport Louisiana by Eric Brock. Includes wonderful photos of the houses and the ladies.

Researching American-Made Toy Soldiers — A 276-page collection of a lifetime of articles by toy soldier expert Richard O'Brien.

Reunion in Hell — Volume One of the John H. Knox series of weird stories from the pulps. Introduced by horror expert John Pelan.

Ripped from the Headlines! — The Jack the Ripper story as told in the newspaper articles in the *New York* and *London Times.*

Rough Cut & New, Improved Murder — Ed Gorman's first two novels.

R.R. Ryan Novels — Freak Museum and The Subjugated Beast, two horror classics.

Ruby of a Thousand Dreams — The villain Wu Fang returns in this Roland Daniel novel.

Ruled By Radio — 1925 futuristic novel by Robert L. Hadfield & Frank E. Farncombe.

Rupert Penny Novels — *Policeman's Holiday, Policeman's Evidence, Lucky Policeman, Policeman in Armour, Sealed Room Murder, Sweet Poison, The Talkative Policeman, She had to Have Gas* and *Cut and Run* (by Martin Tanner.) Rupert Penny is the pseudonym of Australian Charles Thornett, a master of the locked room, impossible crime plot.

Sacred Locomotive Flies — Richard A. Lupoff's psychedelic SF story.

Sam — Early gay novel by Lonnie Coleman.

Sand's Game — Spectacular hard-boiled noir from Ennis Willie, edited by Lynn Myers and Stephen Mertz, with contributions from Max Allan Collins, Bill Crider, Wayne Dundee, Bill Pronzini, Gary Lovisi and James Reasoner.

Sand's War — More violent fiction from the typewriter of Ennis Willie

Satan's Den Exposed — True crime in Truth or Consequences New Mexico — Award-winning journalism by the *Desert Journal*.

Satans of Saturn — Novellas from the pulps by Otis Adelbert Kline and E. H. Price

Satan's Sin House and Other Stories — Horrific gore by Wayne Rogers

Secrets of a Teenage Superhero — Graphic lit by Jonathan Sweet

Sex Slave — Potboiler of lust in the days of Cleopatra by Dion Leclerq, 1966.

Sideslip — 1968 SF masterpiece by Ted White and Dave Van Arnam.

Slammer Days — Two full-length prison memoirs: *Men into Beasts* (1952) by George Sylvester Viereck and *Home Away From Home* (1962) by Jack Woodford.

Slippery Staircase — 1930s whodunit from E.C.R. Lorac

Sorcerer's Chessmen — John Pelan introduces this 1939 classic by Mark Hansom.

Star Griffin — Michael Kurland's 1987 masterpiece of SF drollery is back.

Stakeout on Millennium Drive — Award-winning Indianapolis Noir by Ian Woollen.

Strands of the Web: Short Stories of Harry Stephen Keeler — Edited and Introduced by Fred Cleaver.

Summer Camp for Corpses and Other Stories — Weird Menace tales from Arthur Leo Zagat; introduced by John Pelan.

Suzy — A collection of comic strips by Richard O'Brien and Bob Vojtko from 1970.

Tales of the Macabre and Ordinary — Modern twisted horror by Chris Mikul, author of the *Bizarrism* series.

Tales of Terror and Torment #1 — John Pelan selects and introduces this sampler of weird menace tales from the pulps.

Tenebrae — Ernest G. Henham's 1898 horror tale brought back.

The Amorous Intrigues & Adventures of Aaron Burr — by Anonymous. Hot historical action about the man who almost became Emperor of Mexico.

The Anthony Boucher Chronicles — edited by Francis M. Nevins. Book reviews by Anthony Boucher written for the *San Francisco Chronicle, 1942 – 1947*. Essential and fascinating reading by the best book reviewer there ever was.

The Barclay Catalogs — Two essential books about toy soldier collecting by Richard O'Brien

The Basil Wells Omnibus — A collection of Wells' stories by Richard A. Lupoff

The Beautiful Dead and Other Stories — Dreadful tales from Donald Dale

The Best of 10-Story Book — edited by Chris Mikul, over 35 stories from the literary magazine Harry Stephen Keeler edited.

The Black Dark Murders — Vintage 50s college murder yarn by Milt Ozaki, writing as Robert O. Saber.

The Book of Time — The classic novel by H.G. Wells is joined by sequels by Wells himself and three stories by Richard A. Lupoff. Illustrated by Gavin L. O'Keefe.

The Case in the Clinic — One of E.C.R. Lorac's finest.

The Strange Case of the Antlered Man — A mystery of superstition by Edwy Searles Brooks.

The Case of the Bearded Bride — #4 in the Day Keene in the Detective Pulps series

The Case of the Little Green Men — Mack Reynolds wrote this love song to sci-fi fans back in 1951 and it's now back in print.

The Case of the Withered Hand — 1936 potboiler by John G. Brandon.

The Charlie Chaplin Murder Mystery — A 2004 tribute by noted film scholar, Wes D. Gehring.

The Chinese Jar Mystery — Murder in the manor by John Stephen Strange, 1934.

The Cloudbuilders and Other Stories — SF tales from Colin Kapp.

The Compleat Calhoon — All of Fender Tucker's works: Includes *Totah Six-Pack, Weed, Women and Song* and *Tales from the Tower*, plus a CD of all his songs.

The Compleat Ova Hamlet — Parodies of SF authors by Richard A. Lupoff. This is a brand new edition with more stories and more illustrations by Trina Robbins.

The Contested Earth and Other SF Stories — A never-before published space opera and seven short stories by Jim Harmon.

The Crimson Query — A 1929 thriller from Arlton Eadie. A perfect way to get introduced.

The Curse of Cantire — Classic 1939 novel of a family curse by Walter S. Masterman.

The Devil and the C.I.D. — Odd diabolic mystery by E.C.R. Lorac

The Devil Drives — An odd prison and lost treasure novel from 1932 by Virgil Markham.

The Devil of Pei-Ling — Herbert Asbury's 1929 tale of the occult.

The Devil's Mistress — A 1915 Scottish gothic tale by J. W. Brodie-Innes, a member of Aleister Crowley's Golden Dawn.

The Devil's Nightclub and Other Stories — John Pelan introduces some gruesome tales by Nat Schachner.

The Disentanglers — Episodic intrigue at the turn of last century by Andrew Lang

The Dog Poker Code — A spoof of *The Da Vinci Code* by D.B. Smithee.

The Dumpling — Political murder from 1907 by Coulson Kernahan.

The End of It All and Other Stories — Ed Gorman selected his favorite short stories for this huge collection.

The Fangs of Suet Pudding — A 1944 novel of the German invasion by Adams Farr

The Finger of Destiny and Other Stories — Edmund Snell's superb collection of weird stories of Borneo.

The Ghost of Gaston Revere — From 1935, a novel of life and beyond by Mark Hansom, introduced by John Pelan.

The Girl in the Dark — A thriller from Roland Daniel

The Gold Star Line — Seaboard adventure from L.T. Reade and Robert Eustace.

The Golden Dagger — 1951 Scotland Yard yarn by E. R. Punshon.

The Great Orme Terror — Horror stories by Garnett Radcliffe from the pulps

The Hairbreadth Escapes of Major Mendax — Francis Blake Crofton's 1889 boys' book.

The House That Time Forgot and Other Stories — Insane pulpitude by Robert F. Young

The House of the Vampire — 1907 poetic thriller by George S. Viereck.

The Illustrious Corpse — Murder hijinx from Tiffany Thayer

The Incredible Adventures of Rowland Hern — Intriguing 1928 impossible crimes by Nicholas Olde.

The Julius Caesar Murder Case — A classic 1935 re-telling of the assassination by Wallace Irwin that's much more fun than the Shakespeare version.

The Koky Comics — A collection of all of the 1978-1981 Sunday and daily comic strips by Richard O'Brien and Mort Gerberg, in two volumes.

The Lady of the Terraces — 1925 missing race adventure by E. Charles Vivian.

The Lord of Terror — 1925 mystery with master-criminal, Fantômas.

The Melamare Mystery — A classic 1929 Arsene Lupin mystery by Maurice Leblanc

The Man Who Was Secrett — Epic SF stories from John Brunner

The Man Without a Planet — Science fiction tales by Richard Wilson

The N. R. De Mexico Novels — Robert Bragg, the real N.R. de Mexico, presents *Marijuana Girl, Madman on a Drum, Private Chauffeur* in one volume.

The Night Remembers — A 1991 Jack Walsh mystery from Ed Gorman.

The One After Snelling — Kickass modern noir from Richard O'Brien.

The Organ Reader — A huge compilation of just about everything published in the 1971-1972 radical bay-area newspaper, *THE ORGAN*. A coffee table book that points out the shallowness of the coffee table mindset.

The Poker Club — Three in one! Ed Gorman's ground-breaking novel, the short story it was based upon, and the screenplay of the film made from it.

The Private Journal & Diary of John H. Surratt — The memoirs of the man who conspired to assassinate President Lincoln.

The Ramble House Mapbacks — Recently revised book by Gavin L. O'Keefe with color pictures of all the Ramble House books with mapbacks.

The Secret Adventures of Sherlock Holmes — Three Sherlockian pastiches by the Brooklyn author/publisher, Gary Lovisi.

The Shadow on the House — Mark Hansom's 1934 masterpiece of horror is introduced by John Pelan.

The Sign of the Scorpion — A 1935 Edmund Snell tale of oriental evil.

The Singular Problem of the Stygian House-Boat — Two classic tales by John Kendrick Bangs about the denizens of Hades.

The Smiling Corpse — Philip Wylie and Bernard Bergman's odd 1935 novel.

The Spider: Satan's Murder Machines — A thesis about Iron Man

The Stench of Death: An Odoriferous Omnibus by Jack Moskovitz — Two complete novels and two novellas from 60's sleaze author, Jack Moskovitz.

The Story Writer and Other Stories — Classic SF from Richard Wilson

The Strange Case of the Antlered Man — 1935 dementia from Edwy Searles Brooks

The Strange Thirteen — Richard B. Gamon's odd stories about Raj India.

The Technique of the Mystery Story — Carolyn Wells' tips about writing.

The Threat of Nostalgia — A collection of his most obscure stories by Jon Breen

The Time Armada — Fox B. Holden's 1953 SF gem.

The Tongueless Horror and Other Stories — Volume One of the series of short stories from the weird pulps by Wyatt Blassingame.

The Town from Planet Five — From Richard Wilson, two SF classics, *And Then the Town Took Off* and *The Girls from Planet 5*

The Tracer of Lost Persons — From 1906, an episodic novel that became a hit radio series in the 30s. Introduced by Richard A. Lupoff.

The Trail of the Cloven Hoof — Diabolical horror from 1935 by Arlton Eadie. Introduced by John Pelan.

The Triune Man — Mindscrambling science fiction from Richard A. Lupoff.

The Unholy Goddess and Other Stories — Wyatt Blassingame's first DTP compilation

The Universal Holmes — Richard A. Lupoff's 2007 collection of five Holmesian pastiches and a recipe for giant rat stew.

The Werewolf vs the Vampire Woman — Hard to believe ultraviolence by either Arthur M. Scarm or Arthur M. Scram.

The Whistling Ancestors — A 1936 classic of weirdness by Richard E. Goddard and introduced by John Pelan.

The White Owl — A vintage thriller from Edmund Snell

The White Peril in the Far East — Sidney Lewis Gulick's 1905 indictment of the West and assurance that Japan would never attack the U.S.

The Wizard of Berner's Abbey — A 1935 horror gem written by Mark Hansom and introduced by John Pelan.

The Wonderful Wizard of Oz — by L. Frank Baum and illustrated by Gavin L. O'Keefe

Through the Looking Glass — Lewis Carroll wrote it; Gavin L. O'Keefe illustrated it.

Time Line — Ramble House artist Gavin O'Keefe selects his most evocative art inspired by the twisted literature he reads and designs.

Tiresias — Psychotic modern horror novel by Jonathan M. Sweet.

Tortures and Towers — Two novellas of terror by Dexter Dayle.

Totah Six-Pack — Fender Tucker's six tales about Farmington in one sleek volume.

Tree of Life, Book of Death — Grania Davis' book of her life.

Triple Quest — An arty mystery from the 30s by E.R. Punshon.

Trail of the Spirit Warrior — Roger Haley's saga of life in the Indian Territories.

Two Kinds of Bad — Two 50s novels by William Ard about Danny Fontaine

Two Suns of Morcali and Other Stories — Evelyn E. Smith's SF tour-de-force

Ultra-Boiled — 23 gut-wrenching tales by our Man in Brooklyn, Gary Lovisi.

Up Front From Behind — A 2011 satire of Wall Street by James B. Kobak.

Victims & Villains — Intriguing Sherlockiana from Derham Groves.

Wade Wright Novels — *Echo of Fear, Death At Nostalgia Street, It Leads to Murder* and *Shadows' Edge*, a double book featuring *Shadows Don't Bleed* and *The Sharp Edge.*

Walter S. Masterman Novels — *The Green Toad, The Flying Beast, The Yellow Mistletoe, The Wrong Verdict, The Perjured Alibi, The Border Line, The Bloodhounds Bay, The Curse of Cantire* and *The Baddington Horror.* Masterman wrote horror and mystery, some introduced by John Pelan.

We Are the Dead and Other Stories — Volume Two in the Day Keene in the Detective Pulps series, introduced by Ed Gorman. When done, there may be 11 in the series.

Welsh Rarebit Tales — Charming stories from 1902 by Harle Oren Cummins

West Texas War and Other Western Stories — by Gary Lovisi.

What If? Volume 1, 2 and 3 — Richard A. Lupoff introduces three decades worth of SF short stories that should have won a Hugo, but didn't.

When the Batman Thirsts and Other Stories — Weird tales from Frederick C. Davis.

Whip Dodge: Man Hunter — Wesley Tallant's saga of a bounty hunter of the old West.

Win, Place and Die! — The first new mystery by Milt Ozaki in decades. The ultimate novel of 70s Reno.

Writer 1 and 2 — A magnus opus from Richard A. Lupoff summing up his life as writer.

You'll Die Laughing — Bruce Elliott's 1945 novel of murder at a practical joker's English countryside manor.

RAMBLE HOUSE

Fender Tucker, Prop.   Gavin L. O'Keefe, Graphics

www.ramblehouse.com   fender@ramblehouse.com

228-826-1783   10329 Sheephead Drive, Vancleave MS 39565

www.ingramcontent.com/pod-product-compliance
Lightning Source LLC
Chambersburg PA
CBHW022128080426
42734CB00006B/270